I0626992

Sailing the Sea of Dreams

Coming Home to Your Inner Wisdom

by Judith Schafman, PhD

Sailing the Sea of Dreams
Coming Home to Your Inner Wisdom

By Judith Schafman

Published/Designed :	Nicasio Press
	Sebastopol, California
	www.nicasiopress.com
Artwork & Cover Art:	Judith Schafman
Photographer:	Larry Schafman

ISBN: 979-8-9864100-0-5
Printed in the U.S.A.

We are always on our way from darkness to light.
John O'Donohue, *Walking in Wonder*

DEDICATION

To Larry

Contents

FOREWORD

When reading Dr. Judith Schafman's inspiring book, *Sailing the Sea of Dreams*, one will quickly discover that she has artfully braided together her spiritual journey with many years of study and love of dreams. She has capably offered guidance regarding how to explore the deeper meaning—as well as the significance—of the dreaming process without heavily laden theoretical analysis and scientific terminology.

C. G. Jung suggested that often the dream is its own interpretation. In a similar vein, Dr. Schafman has set the stage by suggesting we allow dream images to speak to us, to come alive, by encouraging the reader to honor dreams through a "recognition practice to be out of your mind and its concoctions and into your ever-opening fresh experience." Furthermore, she recommends the dreamer to steep their dream images like a cup of tea until an "aha" moment emerges—applying an innovative metaphor that the dream serves like a GPS that can potentiate an inner and outer navigational direction.

Entering Dr. Schafman's imaginal world, we are reminded that we are part of the natural world, one with the trees, plants, and animals; and with this sacred awareness we can live closer to our own true nature. This deep knowing of the true self is expressed in the symbolic language of the dream. Antonio Machado, a mystical Spanish poet wrote, "Be aware of the one who walks next to you— the one you tend not to be." This valuable aspect of oneself is waiting to be discovered in the hidden shadows of our dreams. Dr. Schafman has skillfully offered time-tested creative methods to illuminate "the one you tend not to be" so as to make friends with, enhance a more intimate relationship with, and integrate this split-off part of oneself in the service of wholeness.

Rob Sanducci, PhD
Tivoli, NY 2022

PART I

CHAPTER 1:
UNEXPECTED ARRIVAL IN DREAMLAND

Amidst a college teaching career as a professor of psychology, an auspicious and impactful event occurred. Larry (whom I later married) phoned one day and described the dreamwork he had just completed in his therapy group and then offered to work in this same way with a dream of mine. Having just moved into a new apartment, and munching away on donuts and coffee precariously balanced on a trunk, I said, "Sure." A few seconds after my dreamwork with him, I slid to the floor, shocked to see myself crying profusely. There I was, catapulted back into the dream in a surprising, totally unexpected way and sitting in the middle of its meanings. I was profoundly struck by the power of this dreamwork and its ability to rapidly connect me to my own deep feelings and inner life wisdom.

My own childhood had brought forth a love and delight of active imagination. Like many children, I lived in my self-made dreams and worlds for quite some time before entering into what I, with true Peter Pan perspective, anticipated would be boring, magic-free, rules-oriented consensus reality. A young girl, avid reader, and lover of the local library, I traveled into C. S. Lewis's world of Narnia ruled by the great lion, Aslan, and into Edgar Rice Burroughs's African jungle to meet the astounding character Tarzan and the lion, giraffe, gorilla, and elephant inhabitants who lived there. Later on, now as an adult, still searching for something, and still hesitant to join reality—whatever that seemed to be—I journeyed into J.R.R. Tolkien's Middle Earth and the *Lord of the Rings*, and continued looking for other worlds in fantasy and science fiction.

This reluctant adult who spent so much time in imaginative reality finally landed in waking reality, thanks in part to therapeutic explorations and dreamwork with clients on their own unique journeys. How astounding that adulthood offered me, in my work as a therapist and spiritual counselor, an opportunity to explore and have profound and meaningful adventures in other people's dream worlds. There, color, creativity, deep meaning, and unexpected surprises always awaited me. My own life adventure took another unexpected turn when I spent several years living and working in a meditation retreat site, where I finally found the name of my life journey: exploring the self through meditation. My work assignments involved visits to Africa, Japan, Australia, and India, where I worked closely with people living there. As I become familiar with their cultures, daily life issues, and families, my concern for people in different parts of the world expanded exponentially, and I became, in my heart and soul, a global citizen.

Sometime after my surprising dreamwork with Larry, I became a student in a self-designed, creative PhD program offered by Ohio-based Union Graduate School. This unusual degree program had, as its core focus, the student generating her own study by choosing courses from any number of places and self-appointing advisors and teachers. Apart from individual consultations with an advisor, the core of my study included several years of training in a Gestalt Institute in California and more years at a Gestalt Institute in Washington, DC. The Gestalt approach to psychotherapy has as its core the immediacy and healing power of direct experience, doing psychological work fully in the present moment, and enlivening life problems and personality issues through active imagination, psychodrama, and role play. The dreamwork approach described in

Sailing the Sea of Dreams has these Gestalt principles as its foundation.

During my Gestalt Training in California with Erv and Miriam Polster, well-known experts in Gestalt therapy, I had (a) what Jung called a *Big Dream* and (b) fell in love with the dream world. This dream offered profound new directions and meanings for my life, unfolding in many events following its appearance all those years ago. The dream made its importance known with a title and scrolled itself down on the inner dream screen like the beginning of the *Star Wars* movies! Never again did any of my dreams show up with a title, although I did take to titling many myself.

DREAM: THE SUN IS DYING

I and two others are in a tall tower, windows looking out on all sides. We are scrambling around, moving fast and in crisis mode. We knew the sun, that constant external source of light for this world, was dying and would soon fade completely. The tall tower was filled with books that we feverishly gathered up and packed before this event happened. I look up and out a window and see a field below with a solitary man plowing with his ox. The field is bathed in soft blue light. I then am startled—the event has already happened. The sun is gone, and blue light, the new source of illumination, is drenching the scene below.

(Scene changes) I am now at a crossroads in the desert, hills of sand as far as the eye can see, and in extreme heat. A Roman general in full armor is standing at the crossroads. Then up comes a wild, beautiful Native American Indian woman on horseback. The man quickly steps towards the horse, injects it with poison, and it dies on the spot. The woman, furious, unbelieving, weeping, attacks him physically, and screams at him while he fights her off.

(Scene changes.) I myself am a thin man in ragged, simple clothes walking away from the crossroads and down a country road towards Paris. I am on a mission to rescue someone. When I arrive in the city, I go directly to a huge stone castle and enter, clearly knowing what I am doing. I stride up several stone staircases to the top floor. I have unstoppable strong focus upon rescuing a woman being held captive there. I pass the armored man who owns the castle—the one who has imprisoned her. He does nothing to stop me. I find the woman in a room, which is at the top of a turret and has windows in all directions. I see she is sitting on a bed, looking bewildered, as though she doesn't know where she is. As I look at her, an amazing array of mysterious material, a soft substance made up of all colors of the rainbow, emanates from her body, flying out of her and filling the room.

When you read this brief summary you can sense the issues, challenges, and conflicts it presents. What is this life-changing event that the dream people are preparing for? This event in which the light of the world drastically changes? The daylight, ordinary reality revealed by the phases of the sun, now replaced by blue light. Who is this uncompromising Roman General, powerful, organized, militaristic, a disciplinarian and leader of men, carrying the Roman Eagle, a sign of pure power. And what about the Native American woman, living close to nature, flowing with the seasons, a deep relationship with her horse, a strong sense of personal freedom. The appearance of the beautiful horse, an exquisite part of nature, and a friend to humans, killed off. And this castle owner, protecting and hoarding his treasures. The woman herself, now rescued, with color pouring out of her. A born artist in a city that loves painters? There are big themes in this dream, strong characters with their own personalities, each one an important aspect of my personality, and way more fascinating than any psychological labels I might use to define my issues. Be assured I have explored these dream entities and themes my whole life.

In that same Gestalt therapy training came a second shorter dream, also important for my future study and direction as a therapist and dreamworker.

DREAM: FINDING THE SOURCE OF THE RIVER

I am outside walking in the mountains, where there are green, rich trees flourishing, growing tall and majestic. I come to a very strong river flowing down a mountainside. It has a voice of its own and bubbles, gurgles, moves playfully around rocks embedded in its stony, sandy bed. I begin to walk along the side of the river along a wooded pathway, following the river up to its source. I intuitively know that Jung and the dream world are the source of this rapidly flowing river.

The dream draws out my ever-growing interest in dreams, and sends me on my way to study Carl Jung and other Jungians. Sometime after this dream, I had an inspired conversation with Jungian analyst and Episcopal priest Robert Johnson, author of books about inner work, spirituality, and dreaming. I had always been drawn to his writing, and since he lived in California where my Gestalt training was taking place, I decided to look him up. In a visit with him in his backyard, chairs set up under his olive trees, we had a multifaceted conversation about masculine and feminine energy in dreams. At that point I determined to write about the masculine and feminine in dreams for my PhD dissertation.

Returning from the California training, I began my dissertation work by reading Jung and Johnson, writing, taking notes, finding my way in this massive project. I diligently recalled and recorded my own dreams, thinking to include them in the dissertation. I soon discovered that trying to put the glorious unconscious in the service of my conscious educational agenda was, well, a terrible idea! Waking up two or three times a night to catch all dreams that were coming up was depriving me of sleep and leaving me exhausted. Second, this approach was, I discovered, disrespectful of this deeper psychic region within, and an ineffective way of receiving and working with the dreams.

Beginning my own Jungian therapy at the same time, I was told by my new analyst to stop dream recall and to turn my dream journals over to him for at least three months. I was way too attached to them, and was actually drowning in dream material. Well, *that* was a great awakening. Right there, at that moment, I began to develop a great respect for—and sought balance within—my own interior workings and my exterior life. It was not ok to have either dominate the other.

Toward the end of the dissertation writing process, another dream summed up what I still see as, for me, a proper relationship to the dream, the dreamwork, and the inner sea of consciousness.

Dream: The Salt Shack by the Sea

I am in the top floor of a tall skyscraper that overlooks the ocean. The apartment I am in has windows on all sides and a gorgeous view. But because I am very high up, I cannot see or experience the sand, winds and waves first hand. I leave the skyscraper and walk down to the beach. There I observe a gray shack on the beach, very close to the tide line. With shutters blowing in the gentle winds, the house is totally permeated with the sea salt from the ocean. Ahh. A perfect place to sit and be with the ocean and its sea weather and creatures.

From the skyscraper heights, I might have a panoramic view of the ocean environs. In the same way, intellectual study provides a useful view from the heights but, while pointing the way to the seashore, does not provide a direct experience of the ocean. I yearned for the direct experience—the sea breeze, the waves crashing at my feet, the wet sand, and the sound of seagulls.

The ocean for me, has always been a powerful and beloved experience as well as an image of my own unconscious and its hidden depths where creative dreaming occurs. Becoming permeated with salt, as this small shack was, is the result of sitting by the sea of the unconscious, so to speak, and becoming drenched and permeated with the winds, smells, and sounds of my own unconscious. This close relationship between myself and the ocean environment is perfect.

These, then, are my first steps on this inner dream journey, and the foundation for my continued, endless love affair with the fascinating, bewildering, hair-tearing, aggravating, scary, and simply marvelous exploration of my own inner dream creations. What a pathway of powerful inner work—psychological and spiritual— lasting for many years up to last night's dream, which was about a red, fast-moving train that...but I digress.

A Life-Changing Experience

My life-long dream exploration is sustained by a regular meditation practice, ongoing for over 40 years, nurtured by the teachings of Indian scriptures and the philosophy of Kashmir Shaivism in particular. Spiritual practices and studies have given me a clear sense of direction and purpose for my self-exploration and growth, and for my work with others. For this reason, I describe below this single, life-changing meditation experience, a champagne bottle broken on the ship keel of my life that launched me into a long journey of inner purification and spiritual growth.

In 1979, several weeks before I took an initial weekend program in meditation in which this event occurred, I had two dreams, which at that time made no sense.

DREAM: THE ATOM BOMB IN THE OCEAN

I'm sitting on a hill by the mighty ocean, the waves rising, swelling, and crashing regularly into shore. I am talking with a newspaper reporter from my home town, Concord, New Hampshire. Sitting beside me, she says calmly, "When the atom bomb drops and generates tremendous waves, all movement will remain in the ocean, fully contained. You are perfectly safe."

DREAM: CHASED BY AN INDIAN MAN

I am running down the sidewalk of a busy city street, hurriedly dashing in between people, mail boxes, and food stands. I am scared as I am being chased by the head, *only* the head, of an Indian man, who is smiling and laughing at me.

I then took the weekend program in meditation with a teacher from India, Swami Muktananda, who had traveled the world teaching meditation. He looked exactly like that head chasing me! During that weekend, I had a completely unexpected, highly energetic, life-changing, awakening experience. This turned out to be the atom bomb of expanded awareness, gently exploding in my life. Only over time was I able to see and experience the tremendous changes that took place within me as a result.

Initial Meditation Experience

The experience, initiated and fully facilitated by Swami Muktananda, took place in deep meditation. Here it is:

> I find myself in pitch black space, exactly like being in the endless outer space that our planet moves in. "Ah," I thought with some relief. "This is where I will go when I die." Then, gradually, ever so gradually, a very dim light appeared, pale yellow, brightening, then quite yellow, then pale orange in color, and then began to shine brighter and brighter. After some time, the whole space was filled with this bright, vivid, scintillating, orange light.

I noted that the orange color was the same color as the sun and the orange robes worn by the meditation teacher.

I often think of this experience as occurring in exactly the same way that a dimmer switch on the wall works—bit by bit the light goes on. And only bit by bit did I come to understand the experience and its impact on me.

In the thoughts and contemplations about this experience over the next years, I came to see that in my life, there always *is* a step-by-step turning up of the light. I learn to seek and contain the light in the form of the ancient and powerful teachings offered by the brilliant yogi who taught me meditation. To recognize the divinity and sacredness in every person. To meet other people with loving intention and attention. Finally, to see everything—animate and inanimate—as one, all made from the same loving energy. Living into these teachings is a lifetime of work, contemplation, and growth, happening only gradually, over time.

My purpose in life, contemplated and refined over the years, is to seek the loving light of awareness, to turn on this light within myself, and to help others do the same. I came to love the image of a lighthouse, forever moving her light beams over the dark seas, helping those, including myself, sailing out there through rough waters, storms, rocks, and other sea weather, to the safe haven of the shore. The more I can turn on the light in myself, the more I can help the light shine in others. Dreams are light-filled events in themselves, beacons occurring within each person, and leaving light in their wake. Dreamwork then became a strong way that I could personally help others in their search for light.

Lighthouse in Blue

The Purpose of This Book

This book is a memoir of my interior experiences, the many things that happened in my dreams, the people and creatures I met, the dream events I experienced, what I learned, and what I then did about it all in daily life.

Simply speaking, I have throughout my life, befriended my dreams. By seeing how I have welcomed and integrated the inspired wisdom flowing through the people, events, and issues from the dream world, you also can consider doing the same.

The book will also offer those of you who may not have explored dreams in the past some easeful steps to welcome and work with your own nightly dream creations. There is a bibliography at the end of the book for you to refer to when you wish to make a more detailed or theoretical study of dream theories. Here we will not be focusing on dream theory or history. All such information is well worth reading and studying and will later provide an intellectual foundation for your work.

This book also includes my own paintings of special images that emerged from dreams and inner visions. Many are referred to in the text. While gazing at these paintings you may have tiny dream experiences of your own.

Through sharing my experience, I hope you will then choose to look at your own dreams, learn your own personal dream language, and then see how you might apply your learning to your daily life. Please refrain from using what dream symbology books tell you about any image you might have had in a dream. Rather find out for yourself what it means for you. Even Carl Jung, the greatest student of the dream, would tell himself (paraphrased language) at the beginning of his sessions with people, "Carl, you don't know what any dream means." This was his way of supporting the dreamer in his/her own explorations and preventing himself from laying his huge understandings and interpretations on other people's inner worlds.

Dream research from sleep labs does show that every person dreams two to four times every night of life, whether we remember or not. Dreaming is something we have been given as part of "human being equipment" when we came down to Earth. We are certainly sorting out, with daily practice and efforts, how to use our various body parts and our array of mental capacities, but have we sorted out what dreams are for? Now is your chance.

You may find that the GPS that you so easily rely on in your car or on your phone is actually available to you for your personal life via your dreams. Dreams can be an internal GPS. It, along with some experiential study, could help you through life's challenges; give you an experience of your own depth, intelligence, and creativity; give you guidance when you are in tough life situations; inspire you; help release you from past patterns no longer needed; teach you about the beauty of this world; give you the experience of entering new worlds of your own creation; and even connect you with the Higher Power. Welcome to my memoir of personal dream stories!

CHAPTER 2:
YOUR RELATIONSHIP WITH DREAMS

What is your ongoing attitude towards your dreams? Do you simply not notice them? Do you believe that you do not dream? Do you dislike your dreams because they arrive in a jumbled, incoherent, or scary fashion? Are you drowned by the number of dreams that come and want little to do with this tidal wave of imagery? Have you concluded that they are simply of no value, and that even if they were, you would not know what to do with them? And no, you will not be going to a therapist to find out? These waking state attitudes towards dreams considerably shape your dreamwork experience and your potential friendship with your dreams.

Perhaps you do accept dreams but believe that your waking analytical mind can and should be figuring them out. You may even Google the meaning of your images. However, when you conceptualize, explain, like, dislike, or try to judge the dream's importance, you distance yourself from its living energy and your immediate experience in it. Conceptualization and explanation, etc., are processes associated with the workings of your waking mind and thoughts, very necessary and useful but not initially in this situation. The information you hold intellectually can come in as a useful tool after the experiential work with the dream is completed.

Fully experiencing the dream as a living entity without dragging along your preconceived notions and gluing them onto the dream itself takes you into the power of the dream's present-moment live action. At present, I have a sturdy and respectful relationship with my dreams. They come up in the morning when they do, and it's fine when they don't. I write most of them down, sometimes on scraps of paper in the middle of the night, and then paste them into my dream journal. I do dreamwork on those that seem to demand attention and re-read the others with interest. Sometimes the message of the dreams I have not worked on just float to the surface of my awareness in useful ways. Occasionally I wake up with a tune-like "O Happy Day" playing in my awareness, like a song on a radio station. I figure the tune says something about how that inner space that is *me* is feeling! I sheepishly confess: I very frequently think I know what my dream means and then remind myself that I do not know until I let the dream itself speak in some way.

Viewing Dreams as Gifts From Spirit

It is not only important to look at what your relationship with dreams happens to be. It is just as important to look at how you define/experience the inner space. Close your eyes. There you are, in your awareness, *as* the inner space that is you, *in* the inner space. That is where you live.

Here is a proposal. The mysterious inner realms within your being can be seen as sanctified by having Spirit housed there. Some call the dream, an entity born in this inner space, *God's Forgotten Language* (John Sanford). So, when you turn within, to these unknown regions, imagine you are walking through the doorway of a church, synagogue, sweat lodge, or stepping into the deep, green forests or onto sandy ocean shores. When you begin work with a dream, recall and honor its origins.

Further, land in and connect to the life force in your dream because a feeling, thinking, moving energy generates the images and dream stories. The energy behind the image intelligently crafts the image it wants to show up in. The message of the dream is designed especially for you at that moment in time.

There is a delightful Mexican custom in which children at their birthday parties are blindfolded, then jump around and enthusiastically whack away at a container called a *piñata* hanging on a tree by a rope, until the gifts it contains spill out in a colorful array onto the ground. This playful activity is a very good description for working with the energy of a dream image, although we don't actually have to whack away at it like the kids in this example. But we do talk about it, poke it, stand in it, be it, speak as it, dramatize it, and play around in it! Soon there is a piñata-like explosion, large or small, of the energy and gift of meaning inside that image, which then arrives in our awareness.

What follows is an important personal encounter with my dreams when I had not been in regular touch with them for some time and did not consider them of immediate importance. Here is what happened and what I did about it.

DREAM: THE BLUE-TOOTHED SNAKE BITES MY HAND

I walk through a bed of fallen, crumpling autumn leaves in a dried-out forest. Everything is dead, waiting for the soft, white, winter snow. I come upon a huge snake who is dying and would need nourishment badly to live. I carefully walk around him, as his size is frightening, and then find a pyramid of grains to feed him. As I offer him these pellet-like grains, he starts to regain his energy. He opens his mouth and with lightning speed, bites my hand with his huge, blue tooth (no, not that kind of bluetooth!) before I can run away. I wake up frightened and awed.

The dream did pose important questions that I knew I needed to attend to. What energy does this huge snake carry? How would this dream snake get so dried out? Be close to death, even? The answer was not so mysterious. I had been involved in a demanding job, getting up quite early each morning and had not recalled or worked on dreams for a very long time when the above dream arrived. I came to see that with little thought to my own interior nature, both psychological and spiritual, all my color and intuitive knowledge could dry up or be covered over with the dry leaves of forgetfulness or false priorities.

And it is not just ignoring dreams that is the problem. It is ignoring all the skillful means available to live from inside of yourself, including prayer, meditation, yoga, other spiritual practices, journaling, therapy, painting, and consciousness-raising of any kind. Without these activities that help us turn within, we stay caught up in the outer story of our lives and regularly miss the larger question and experience of who we really are.

After the active dreamwork with this unusual snake, I then did some research. Noticing that this snake became quite alive with only a little bit of food from this pyramid of grains, I looked up "pyramid." Pyramid is a seventeenth-century symbol for alchemy, the ancient system for spiritual transformation in which the so-called "lead" of an unexamined life is turned into "gold" of conscious awareness. The light of this golden awareness certainly applied to what was needed in my current state. I did need to bring much more awareness to what I truly needed at this time.

In Kundalini Yoga, the spiritual energy called Kundalini is said to be like a snake, coiled at the base of the spine and moving serpent-like up the chakras, cleaning and purifying as it goes through the practice of meditation. This dream suggests purifying/ nurturing myself via more and deeper meditation. The snake bite for me generated the new-found, strong desire to go way deeper into myself to discover what was truly inside. So, I did.

Now I leave you with the question, what is *your* relationship with dreaming? Or, as important, your relationship with any other practice that feeds and expands your own deep awareness?

Chapter 3:
The Whispers of Mystery

It is rare that a dream arrives offering a message you are already totally familiar with. It does occasionally happen that a dream is a replay of the previous day, but even in that case, it is likely you will learn something new about how you see daily life.

Every dream arrives from the hidden spaces of mystery and then with dreamwork, revelation occurs. Over and over, year after year, dream stories and entities fully surprise me with who they reveal themselves to be and what they have come to say to me about my life.

Dreams will take you to places you have never been before. Embrace your own curiosity and courage, and be willing to open the doors to this mystery. Stand in front of its darkness and hidden promise. I believe that there is a drive within you that demands revelation, to see within and know yourself as deeply as you can. Hafiz, the divine Persian poet says (in *I Heard God Laughing* by Danial Ladinsky): "Hafiz can stand on a blessed peak inside his heart and see for hundreds of years in all directions." Looking deeply within "in all directions" at your dreams can be part of the blessed journey toward the "Ancient One" that Hafiz and other great poet saints speak of.

The Unknown and the Familiar

Don Juan, a Yaqui Shaman teacher, was made popular many years ago in a series of books (see especially *The Eagle's Gift*) written by Carlos Castaneda, a California sociologist. Don Juan explains the unknown to his recalcitrant pupil, Carlos, in some impactful teaching conversations. He places salt and pepper shakers and a sugar bowl around on the checkered tabletop cloth in a tiny Mexican café while they are having lunch.

The salt and pepper shakers represent what Don Juan calls the "tonal," the ordinary things in life, the things that can be seen and of which we know the function. The space outside of the tabletop is called the *nagual* or the spacious mystery, the place out of which all sorts of powerful, unexpected events emerge.

He goes on to say that we have experiences of both these places on a continuous basis, whether we know it or not. We live our lives on that tabletop of familiarity, in what we know and are comfortable with. Roads, cities, snowy weather, internet glitches, work projects, birthday parties, global warming, politics, football, best friends, cell phones, cars, raising kids, relatives coming and going, life goals, intentions, dreams, feelings, problems, etc., and etc.!

But this place of familiarity with all its items, as Don Juan points out, has the waters of the unknown and unpredictable lapping at its edges and underneath all its sides. Synchronicities, visions, chance but highly important meetings, longed for events that suddenly occur, "aha" experiences, déjà vu, predictive dreams, intuitions, surprising and unexpected occurrences, and many more come from the spacious mystery.

As I am writing this chapter, my husband, Larry, has a surprising daily experience occur, a wrong number call that has a depth of sweetness to it that touches his heart. The young boy calling says, "Hello, grandfather, I'm your youngest grandchild!" This is very warmhearted, but Larry has no grandchildren. However, as a reporter for the local school system, he sees himself as celebrating children in his work and dearly loves every child he photographs as though they were his own. The child's sweet phone call gives him surprising acknowledgment and makes heartfelt sense as the experience emerges out of the wrong number magic and the mystery of the moment.

As much time as we spend learning to know the dream, to visit it, to move in and unlock its secrets, these dream stories and entities will never be comfortable living-room furniture on that table of familiarity. They will always arrive, enigmatic, often unclear but always presenting an invitation to move further into our own unknown depths, and to open the door to revelation.

Since the dream is itself elusive, we can be creative in our approach. Our active imagination flows in and out of the forms of the dream, making up dialogue and meaning in much the same way that a writer works on and refines dialogue for a film or play. If we develop a fluid, unpredictable approach to the dream, bending and dancing with it, then we have actually practiced how to approach the unknown, and the dream as its offspring.

An author friend of mine, who is in the middle of writing adventure stories about five children, commented that her creations, these children, have now taken on lives of their own and surprise her with what they say and do. Another author friend has several books full of people who travel around the world having unimaginable meetings and adventures, and he shares he never knows what they will be up to next. Dreamwork moves in this same unpredictable way. While all dreams contain mystery, what follows are dreams with the energy of the unknown quite strong.

DREAM OF THE UNICORN

I am in a forest, leaning on a huge rock. As I look down the hill, I see a unicorn walking softly, quietly in and out of the trees.

While having worked on this dream months before, I recently returned to it in the midst of a lecture I was giving on how to work with dreams. As a way of teaching the students dreamwork methods, I playfully became the unicorn and asked the audience to question *me-as-unicorn* in order to discover a bit about my nature.

Speaking as the unicorn, I say: "I am filled with presence and ancient magic, a creature living and yet found only in imagination. I am full of the unknown yet wanting to be known. And wanting to live in this world."

As I later ponder these words, I realized that to be fully present is the unicorn's true nature. More astounding, I realized I, as unicorn, was walking, moving, and speaking as my soul. Would I ever know the nature of my own soul? I hold this unicorn presence delicately, carefully, hoping to watch it unfold and over time, reveal even further its true nature.

DREAM: THE COUNTRY CALLED "I DON'T KNOW"

I am walking down a beach not knowing where I am or where I am going. I see and walk by hundreds of empty but colorful beach cottages near the ocean shore and see a train station in the distance. I go towards the station.

As a participant in a dream group at that time, I work on the dream content. But even with the work, I still have no idea what is going on. Nothing came except "I don't know." It was as though I had amnesia in the dream itself. I simply could not connect with emotion, meaning, or any of the people or story, yet I seemed to be taking various actions in the actual dream itself.

The dream therapist, sticking very close to my unfolding process, asks me to explore the country called "I don't know." What a great idea. I stand and begin moving around the room, stepping into this mysterious country. It seemed to be a place of creative expression with all the materials fully present. Like a Santa's workshop, or a divine art studio. I could, with great delight, create whatever I wanted while in this place of unknowing. It would all just flow with no effort.

I then stop conversing with the therapist and sit on the floor. I now have no thought and move into a deeper, quiet state, aware of the present moment. The "I don't know" delivers me to a meditative space, completely filled with presence, and there I feel my power as a meditator. What a fully unexpected place to land.

We are frequently in life situations where we simply don't know. Often, we think or want to know, pretend that we know but really do not. We may not know what to do or think. We definitely don't know what will happen. Look at what can happen if we sit in the middle of the "I don't know" experience.

"I Don't Know" Postscript

Years later, my husband Larry and I were on September holiday at our favorite Maine beach. One morning we found a small place for breakfast, owned by local residents who took great delight in their breakfast concoctions. We were seated at a table underneath a painting, which, wow!, had in it the exact image of my dream with the many colorful empty cottages. I had such delight in seeing these old friends.

Many more years passed since running into a photo of those colorful cottages at that breakfast place. As I began work on this book, I recalled the gray shack (see chapter 1) appearing in the beginning year of my dreamwork while I was working on my PhD. That old gray dream shack had been the perfect place to sit while watching the sea of dreams in front of me. Oh! Yes. That gray shack had over the years been transformed into many colorful cottages on the beach—fresh images of where I've been seated during all the years of my color-filled dreamwork. And there today I still sit.

I delight in seeing how the soul keeps track of itself, expresses itself and its development with its own images, and communicates to me up here in waking reality so that I can delight in this interior process.

Some questions for you to ponder are:

What are the life items on your table of familiarity? I, with great familiarity, have eaten grapefruit, eggs, and an English muffin every morning of my life, and my route to the grocery store remains the same day in and day out. I do like these particular routines, so no need to make them wrong.

On the other hand, what is unanswerable, unknown, or mysterious in your life, nipping at your heels, wanting to be looked at? For me, there are mundane questions like, will I ever get to Maine again for my ocean holiday? When will I see my new great-nephew, Maximus? There are also larger questions concerning the unknown: *What happens when we die? Where do we actually go?*

How do you position yourself and what do you tell yourself in relation to these things? Are you in a friendship with the unknown?

∞

CHAPTER 4:
DREAMS EMERGE FROM SHADOWS

Do any of the following sound familiar?

- I had such an upsetting dream last night, so miserable I wish I didn't remember it. It's probably because I (a) didn't sleep well, (b) had rich food for dinner—pizza will kill me yet, or (c) had a fight with my co-worker in the office, or even (d) my credit card is so maxed out, I am worried sick.

- I've had this dream over and over, and it's ruining my sleep. I don't even want to go to bed. I'll take a sleep aid, and with any luck I'll forget it.

- In my dream I'm (a) missing the elevator; (b) losing my keys, phone, laptop, wallet, purse; (c) late for a meeting, a class, my graduation or wedding; (d) forgetting where I parked my car. Anxiety, anxiety, and more anxiety. I really don't need nights like this. Lately days are bad enough.

- Sometimes my dreams come true the next day. I don't like that and don't know why it happens to me. Is there something wrong with me, or is this some hidden talent I have? I'm going to try to ignore all of them.

In all of the examples, the bad or weird dream is getting a bad rap. I still recall a dream of a green, square-shaped creature with beady red eyes living behind the walls in my house, his presence scaring me to death. I won't go into its story right now.

These upsetting dreams, including nightmares, can carry the most powerful messages of growth for us. All dreams contain what we have disavowed, avoided, refused to look at, or had no knowledge of. Nightmares, and recurring dreams in particular, carry important, disavowed shadow material. The shadow archetype, a label given to this dark material by Carl Jung, is defined in Robert Johnson's book *Owning Your Own Shadow* as "that which has not entered adequately into consciousness."

Simply stated, we have not let the issue that generated the dream rise up into waking awareness. These dreams come up in scary forms because they have tried over and over to come up in meaningful, nicer forms. But we didn't listen or pay attention or even know we should. In the scary form, finally they get our attentions. So, pay attention. What follows is a brief explanation of what might contribute to these shadow dreams.

All cultures and families offer up social conditioning and traditions that dictate standards to its children regarding how to think, feel, behave, and what to be ashamed of and proud of. Without conscious thought, we swallow and follow the invisible byways and highways of the cultural correctness code, displaying socially approved behaviors and feelings so we can be accepted.

We suppress or deny the thoughts, feelings, behaviors, and experiences that don't fit the code and are deemed threatening to our well-being or acceptance by others.

Or, consciously or unconsciously, we rebel against the code, still being run by it in our rebellion. With no awareness, we can try, in our discomfort, to get disapproved-of thoughts and behaviors out of our own insides by projecting them onto someone else. We then see *that* person displaying the very traits we are so unwittingly uncomfortable with inside. Last, at any time in our lives, there may be inner or outer experiences that are so uncomfortable and painful that we sidestep, ignore, or just plain suppress them.

Suffice to say, this unclaimed baggage drags us down. While repression may have been a fully appropriate way of handling things earlier in our life, if too long denied or not consciously acknowledged, things can burst through into consciousness in the form of intense unpredictable emotion (road rage, extreme anger towards others), unruly or destructive behavior (the many forms of violence directed to self or others), and body symptoms, (psoriasis, chronic fatigue, and worse). And as we have just pointed out, the unclaimed baggage can easily take the form of disturbing dreams.

The following dreams, my own and those shared by clients, demonstrate these points.

DREAM: TWELVE TALKING TOILETS

An embarrassed woman shared a dream of being trapped in a ladies' room containing twelve filthy toilets, which she was supposed to clean. It was overwhelming, disgusting, and a mess.

Yes, this dream was quite a visual picture of the state of her psychic basement.

In her dreamwork, she allowed each of the twelve toilets to speak (i.e., I am toilet number one and here is what I have to say...), and they had a lot to say. Yes, she did have to clean up her own shit. Yes, there were many messes in her life she had turned away from and not attended to: trouble with family, shaky finances, a marriage beset with issues, etc. While this dream brought it all up into awareness and was a big confrontation, believe it or not, the dream came with some very humorous, light-hearted energy. Talking to twelve toilets is bound to generate some laughter! And once the "shit" was brought up into awareness, options and choices began to naturally present themselves to her.

DREAM: BEING RELENTLESSLY PURSUED

A woman had a recurring dream in which an unknown man was chasing her through New York City, through alleyways, up and down the stairs in skyscrapers, in the subway, into her place of work. Everywhere she went or tried to escape, there he was.

In this case, the issues and feelings hidden in the shadows came up in the form of a recurring dream. Recurring dreams, by the way, are recurring invitations to handle something very important to one's well-being and peace. She was terrified, and because the dream happened over and over, she began to feel an aversion to sleep.

When she finally allowed the dream man to speak to her, (it took courage, to actually step into this image and feel its energy) she was shocked. He did not want to kill her or harm her in any way. He said he was her man, her masculine energy, and that she needed him desperately to solve some difficult, on-going problems in her work and life. Enough being so wishy-washy, refusing to assert herself, refusing to "be a man." Time to integrate the masculine energy as her own. The whole issue was terribly uncomfortable for her, but she plunged ahead.

It's not surprising: facing into the shadow and doing the work required is uncomfortable and downright challenging. The sparks and tears fly. And, sometimes deep-seated, painful issues and experiences are revealed. In these cases, you may wish to choose carefully which kinds of healing modalities to use. Experiential dreamwork, with its strong energy releases, may not be your best choice.

A woman, who is at first reluctant to work with her upsetting dream, shares the following:

Dream: The Cat Who Didn't Drown

I am weeping hysterically and crying when I see that my beloved cat has fallen into a pond and is sinking to the bottom and drowning. It is too late for me to save him.

When she allows the cat to speak for itself in the dreamwork, the cat says: "I have not drowned at all. I am sinking into a quiet place within myself to meditate. Please face into your need for stillness, so helpful to your health and well-being. Please. Meditate."
She did.
This is an example of taking the surface story of the dream as truth, being afraid and too emotionally upset to look at the hidden meanings, which might be deeply beneficial to you.

Burying Gold

It is not only that we bury what is unpleasant or painful to us. People mysteriously hide their finest qualities and talents in the shadows. Examples are endless—compassion, understanding, love, unexpressed or undeveloped talents, latent or hidden potentials, artistic, athletic, musical and writing abilities, a healing or legal bent, and on and on.

Is there an unexpressed fear of stepping out of our self-generated safety zones? Stepping into our own greatness, talent, magnificent self-expression? Would we be too vulnerable? Frightened of failure? Sometimes we touch into these undeveloped parts of ourselves when we admire those who have the very qualities that we too have but don't own. Also, we may be drawn to read about or participate in events, or make choices that substitute for those unseen qualities within. Hopefully we don't marry a lawyer instead of becoming one ourself. Again, hopefully, we don't just visit art galleries instead of trying our own hand at painting.

DREAM: VAN GOGH IS IN THE BACK SEAT OF MY CAR

I am shocked to see that there are prints and paintings all over the inside of my car, which magically has grown into a huge space. Drawings of trees, nature, people, daughters and mothers, children. On the floor in the back is also a perfect replica of Van Gogh's bedroom painting: the little bed, the wooden chair, his own paintings on the wall.

I am deeply touched. The appearance of Van Gogh's drawings gives me the opportunity to look yet another time at fully owning my painting process and experiencing the delight I find in it. It is not time to focus energy on admiring the artistry of others, even world-famous people, but to know I carry artistry around within myself. I have my own room, with my own paintings on the walls, and that is to be celebrated. No cringing or hiding from my own full self-expression or fearful of being vulnerable, but rather a fully embodied enjoyment of the artistry flowing through me.

So, while dancing on the sunny side of the street is a joy, wandering around on the dark side can yield pure gold, and major expansion in your understanding and appreciation of yourself. In summary, the most frightening nightmares and dark dream scenes can open into brand-new, inspired perspectives and solutions via dreamwork.

Lighthouse in Gray

CHAPTER 5:
DREAMS SHINE FROM HEAVENLY REALMS

Dreams of Spirit can appear in the inner spaces like a ray of light and express through simply divine and inspired imagery. When receiving such a dream, the experience is often one of extreme wonder and gratitude that our deepest self is speaking to us. Dreams of Spirit, directly from the heart, can reveal profound feelings from our best selves like compassion, devotion, love, perseverance, and dedication. These qualities, because they come from soul, show the depth, nature, and goodness of our own being. We may go back to the dream over and over to bathe in its inspiration. We may also continue the work to fully integrate these divine qualities into our own personality.

As well as these divine qualities, dreams of Spirit also can contain surprising insights, needed wisdom arising from the inner depths, and wonder-filled scenes and experiences of tremendous beauty. Sometimes they simply contain great mystery, its meanings not immediately, if ever, revealed. Finally, an inner teacher, in any shape or form, can appear, who comes with direct teaching or important personal truths. What follows are examples of these dreams of Spirit.

Inner wisdom can come in flashes of insight, and suddenly we know something we did not know before, know a way to go we did not see before. Sometimes we can actually hear words being said, hear something sung, see writing, or see an image that contains a direction or a truth we need. Our perspective, washed by the images and wisdom given, expands immediately.

By a woman who is a training consultant and ex-college teacher:

DREAM: CAMPAIGNING FOR OBAMA

I am sitting in a small living room with light brown leather couches in an office building somewhere. Barack Obama sits on a couch directly in front of me and, holding my hand, talks extensively to me. I cannot hear or recall what he says, but I have a tremendously strong, positive feeling towards him.

This dream occurred many months before Barack Obama received the Democratic Party 2008 nomination. The woman who had this dream had not followed or participated in political activities for many years and in fact had voted for Hillary Clinton in the primaries. Months later, she was prompted to travel, to go door-to-door, canvassing voters, surprising herself with her participation and enthusiasm. She also did phone work for the campaign and hosted events that supported others to make phone calls. Sometime during these activities, she recalled her own dream with awe as she watched its inner guidance unfold. She was deeply heartened and moved when Barack Obama won the presidency.

The dreamer realized she had stepped out of the world of her narrow concerns and into the expansive space of global citizenship. Her feeling of deep compassion for the human family, the planet, and its animals grew each day. With old personal cynicisms softened, she also experienced a sense of duty in continuing to offer community service after the campaign.

Barack Obama, for her, carried iconic, transformative energy, a doorway into that larger stance of compassionate and honorable activism. In this first dream of Spirit, we can, as did the dreamer, contemplate ourselves as world citizens offering our energy and service for others in the global living room.

The Appearance of an Inner Teacher

Jesus, Buddha, an accomplished teacher in the arts or in spiritual practices, an animal carrying a special, even magical, ability, a natural force like the ocean, with a voice—powerful and special entities appear to show us something, give a direct teaching, healing, or mirror back something important about ourselves. We have an "aha" experience—for us, unbelievable and so needed—and recognize the truth that is being given.

From Larry, my husband, who is a public relations person in a school system, an historian, and community worker:

DREAM: A MODERN-DAY ODYSSEY

I am in a group where people are studying excerpts from *The Odyssey,* a book about a hero's journey. Everyone in the class is reading different versions of this profound text.

My spiritual teacher enters the room, goes around and asks people to read from their text. I am following my page, though it is challenging, because the words I am reading are different from the version the current reader has. Also, my version is hand-written, and some words are barely legible. After the class, I am given the keys to a black sedan, which I then back out of a driveway and onto a street. The driveway is difficult to maneuver, particularly if I tried to pull out backward. I have to turn the car completely around. When I finally get on the street, I drive forward, the car now having turned into a white convertible!

For ten years after the fall of Troy, Odysseus sailed the seas and had outlandish adventures, including avoiding the deadly Sirens and killing the ferocious Cyclops. The whole journey was a true "hero's adventure." The gods and goddesses debated his future and regularly intervened in his life, especially Athena, the goddess of wisdom and warfare. He finally returned home, killed off all his enemies, set his kingdom right, and reunited with his wife, Penelope. That's the short version.

At the time of the dream, this dreamer was tossed around in his own sea of change. He had been pulled into the rocky and treacherous waters of policies, politics, promises, and ever-changing loyalties in the workplace. Stirred up and uncertain, he constantly contemplated what might be next for him in his life's work. In the dream, instead of backing out onto highway, with only limited vision, and therefore putting himself in danger, he is very cautious. He takes his time and turns around fully, so that he can go forward safely and with full vision.

Spirit here appears as dream wisdom. While not offering specific solutions to his current problems, the dream offers some commentary on what direction to take: *Don't back dangerously onto the highway of choices available to you without looking carefully. Instead, turn your perspectives around and go forward safely in your chariot—a white convertible!*

In this second dream, we can consider that we are not just sludging along in the daily psychodrama. Rather, we are on a courageous Hero's Journey with a high purpose in which the soul is being strengthened and refined as it makes its way towards its own center.

From my art mentor, who is a professional artist and art teacher:

DREAM: THE SKY OF MANY MOONS

I am working on a labyrinth art project on a hillside. As I look up, I see a crescent moon right above the full moon, appearing through the clouds in the south. Then I see a full moon in the east, another one in the north, and one more in the west, as well. This is a momentous occurrence! The sky gets covered up by clouds when I try to show this phenomenon to my wife.

In waking life, the dreamer and his wife had made a garden labyrinth where they grew vegetables for several summer seasons. Since he had embodied the actual experience of labyrinth digging for many days through this project, its energy permeates his daily domestic life and artistic projects.

The labyrinth, a powerful dream image, is a coiled earthwork with a central point. It communicates the complex twists and turns of the journey the dreamer is taking into the inner worlds to discover his true essence or core.

This dream of wonder expands even further. The celestial landscape of four moons in four directions as well as a crescent moon above the full moon to the south is truly astounding. Imagine the actual experience of the dreamer, looking at this magical sky, being shown its message.

Shiva, the chosen deity of this dreamer, is present in every moment, situation, life stage, and in all phases of life, in the same way that the moon has her phases, shapes and seasons. Shiva and his moons let the dreamer know that within him is this Shiva Light, this high, fully illuminated perspective. And the stunningly lit sky, the full moon in every direction, is the state that is given within, so says the dreamwork, as a result of the journey of the labyrinth digging.

The dreamer then says, "When I try to show this phenomenon to my wife, the sky gets clouded up."

In this third dream, we have awakened our sense of wonder and miracles, as we see the profound beauty in this world. We are shown a pathway into our own deepest nature in the form of the labyrinth and touch the state that can be given to us as we deepen our inner work. Finally—and is this not the challenge?—we are invited to bring our spiritual understandings and highest perspectives into daily life interactions with those we love. What a wonder is this dream on every level.

My own dream:

DREAM: A MYSTERY

I see a mountain range in the distance with fires burning all through them and on the top as well. As we watch, the fire gets closer and closer, sparks are flying, and could now be threatening us. Someone puts the sparks out.

While I had many thoughts about the dream meaning and tried to work with it, nothing clicked experientially. I then recalled that the *I Ching* had a hexagram that referred to the elements of fire and earth, and discovered that Hexagram 56 is entitled "Fire on the Mountain." I read the commentary for that hexagram in Brian Walker's *I Ching or Book of Changes*: "We are all wanderers in the Unknown. Those who travel beside the Sage are protected from harm." Staying profoundly connected to the sage (great teacher) who knows his way through the mountains as I travel my life journey is the core teaching of this hexagram.

This *I Ching* commentary certainly captured my experience as I wandered unknowingly about this dream. Further, as was mentioned in the beginning of the book, it supports the notion of embracing mystery and the unknown as it is threaded through our lives and in dreams all the time.

We have visited dreams emanating from the shadows and those that shine with heavenly light. We now continue to look at how to see our personal relationship with dreams and then how to work with dreams in more detail.

Seagull

CHAPTER 6:
SAY HELLO TO YOUR DREAM EGO

In all dreams, there is an "I" present, an aware voice telling the story of the dream event. This "I" in the dream is called the dream ego. It goes by your name, and it seems like the actual dream is happening to this dream ego, called "Judy" (insert your own name here). Further, when recalling the dream, we are actually reporting the perspective of this dream ego. All dreams I have shared here are done so by my saying as I report the dream, "I did this, I did that, I saw this, I felt that."

Sometimes this experience of being the I-awareness could be while you are standing in your own body in the dream or in the body of a giraffe, or in any other creature. In the "Sun is Dying" dream reported to you in chapter 1, my sense of "I" was located in the body of the young, thin man who was walking off to Paris, who then saved the woman in the turret.

The dream ego frequently knows the least about what is going on in the dream compared to the other dream entities, objects, and people. In fact, the dream ego often carries your waking state of limited opinions, fears, and ways of thinking, behaving, and feeling into the dream. Occasionally, the dream ego, protective of its own perspectives, will try to squeeze the dream into superficial, safe understandings no matter how expansive or mysterious the dream might actually be. For example, if as the dream ego, you are running away from all of the monsters in your dream, it is possible that you are running away from the waking-state monsters and difficulties in your waking state.

Here is an example of a fearful, narrow-minded dream ego:

DREAM: THE TUNNEL PROJECT

I am in a verdant green forest in early spring. Throughout the forest is a beautiful park with unusual paintings displayed on stands and trees, and rare flowers blooming. My art mentor invited me to help dig a huge tunnel that would spiral down deep into the earth in the middle of this forest. After digging for a while, he would make paintings along the tunnel walls and then return to the digging. I was very nervous about the project, frightened by the tunnel, and did not want to join in.

If I had believed the perspective represented by my Judy-dream-ego in the above dream and refuse to take the invitation to do the work of painting and digging, I would miss out on a spectacular activity taking place beneath the earth.

Fortunately, the other dream entities got a chance to share their wisdom. They, and most especially the artist, offer experiences that lead to fresh new learning and bright possibilities for me in the waking state. The inner painter here is digging the way down into my own hidden interior and affirming that painting is a strong means of self-reflection for me.

Here is another example of Judy-dream-ego expressing herself, and further commentary from other dream inhabitants.

DREAM: THE GYPSY COMES TO FETCH ME

I am inside a beautiful house in the forest. As I walk down the hall with my large dog who is on a short leash, a colorful-looking gypsy woman pulls up outside in a green Volkswagen. The dog jumps and pulls on his leash, wanting to run out to greet the woman. I will not let him go.

In the following dreamwork, Judy, the gypsy and the dog speak their opinions and feelings:

Judy-dream-ego says: "I am very uncomfortable with this visitor. My dog will stay on the leash, and will not go outside running around and jumping up on a stranger. I will not let this visitor in. I don't know her, and she looks eccentric and weirdly different. So, the dog stays in, and the gypsy woman stays out."

Gypsy speaks: "I am colorful layers of material for creating beautiful works of art. Absorb me fully and paint your life and art in your own creative way. Let loose! Take the adventure I offer. No need to be so-o-o disciplined!"

The dog speaks: "Woof! Woof! Let me out!"

Here I am invited to monitor the short leash I keep myself on and to look at a reluctance to open the door to the new adventures awaiting me. I very much want to express my creativity and take every opportunity to dive into painting. This gypsy, with her multi-layered color and her ability to travel in such a playful way, is exactly the energy I need. Holding myself back is not at all life-affirming.

In conclusion, the dream ego, with the attention given through dreamwork, can actually be educated to what is going on in dreams. She/he can become kinder, smarter, and more helpful in the dream story, and be strengthened in waking life. Following the adventures of dream ego is always, just on its own, a surprising and useful contemplation. Simply pay attention to what the "you" in the dream is up to, on a regular basis, and you will be educated. Ultimately, the existence of the dream ego and her usually narrow perspective is a vital catalyst in the dream that calls forth everyone else in the dream to speak, agree, argue, or offer new perspectives—the full case for inviting everything else in the dream to express themselves

Chapter 7:
Everyday Dreamwork Instructions

The perspective that everything in the dream is a part of you in visual form is the foundation for dreamwork methods presented here. The dream is carved out of your own psyche, made of your own awareness, your own golden consciousness. The images and stories are cut from your deepest feelings, attitudes, fears, joys, and goals, and, as per Jung, even from your culture, and history/archetypes. All is sent to you from the deep realms of your own core.

The Click of Recognition

Arriving at the meaning of an image is not a figuring it out process but a visceral experience, meaning you feel it in your gut. At some point you will have a click of recognition, an "aha" of knowing or a sense of rightness about what was asked and what was said in the dream work. You trip upon a truth about yourself, which you recognize when you hit the meaning of the image. For me, it is like the fizz sound when you pop a coke cap off the bottle!

Recognition becomes stronger and clearer with diligent practice. In fact, the true offerings of dreamwork depend on your developing a sense of recognition for when your dream inhabitants are speaking your truth. For that, you have to be outside of your mind and its concoctions, and into your ever-opening, fresh experience.

The sense of recognition of your own images and their meanings prevents you from getting bogged down in culturally conditioned *associations* to images and wandering all over the place with associations that have nothing to do with you. The road can be tricky here. You can falsely feel that you've hit upon the true meaning, when in fact you might have grabbed for something a bit more comfortable than the still hidden true meaning. Be vigilant. Don't confuse the mind's commentary with the actual dreamwork.

This is the ongoing, hardest practice to take on. You will make mistakes, and you will be delighted when you arrive at your truth.

An Example of the Mind Concocting Associations

I dream of a fantastically powerful red dragon in flight. My mind, full of mental associations and past memories of books I have read and loved, reminds me that the red dragon was a symbol for Pendragon in the King Arthur stories. So therefore, if I dream of a dragon, it is probably telling me that I need a trip to Great Britain? Or perhaps I had a past incarnation in Great Britain during Arthur's time. Well, possible! Or perhaps I am to step into some kind of queen-like leadership role or I am realizing some new magical powers found in the Arthur myth? (Really, Judith?) These thoughts and ideas equate to not going into the dream at all. Rather they represent my clinging to attractive and popular associations floating around in the cultural atmosphere or stories I have made up.

When I actually become the dragon, feel its contour, shape, exactly as it is in my dream, I find the ancient voice of my own wild, imaginative power flapping away with its powerful wings. Now I love this image, and it is mine.

What follows in this chapter as well as in chapters 8 and 9 are various aspects and approaches to dreamwork that will allow you to begin your personal study.

Returning to the Dream

- First, notice any thoughts or opinions you might have about your current dream, and set them aside or drop them.

- With eyes closed, imagine that you can consciously breathe down back into the dream and its images, people, and stories. Notice when you have landed there.

- See the dream scene itself. If you can't see it, then sense, or recall it, or go back to your dream journal and review it. Get the scene in mind in whatever way you can. You are not just recalling the dream; you are re-entering it.

Getting to Know the Dream Inhabitants

Write the Dream Down in your Dream Journal

This seems like a simple step. However, as we are on a mission to befriend our dreams, contribute to the newly forming friendship by picking out a dream journal you really like. Before you get out of bed in the morning, write your dream down, with no worry about how much or how little you remember.

Draw and Sketch any Images from the Dream

Think about getting a journal with unlined pages. You can also purchase colored pens, pencils or crayons. In this way you can use color in your dream recordings. Remember as kids, we would grab the crayons and scribble. Anything. Don't run off into the issue of "I have no drawing talent." Just be a kid with your colored pencils and crayons and scribble away.

Title the Dream

Without much thought, give your chosen dream a title, i.e., "Broadway or Bust," "The Creature Who Lives in the Wall," "Help!"

etc. Take a few moments to determine what that title reminds you of in your life right now. This short and simple practice can begin the journey of getting to the deepest meaning of your dream.

The Adjectives Approach

Turn to a dream in your journal that you are interested in. Make a list of people (college friend, etc.), objects (a dirty couch, etc.), weather (a tornado, etc.), buildings (a skyscraper falling apart, etc.), creatures (a dog, etc.), that appear in your dream. Pick out a few images you are most drawn to, and come up with two or three adjectives that describe the dream image. Next, simply ask yourself what the dream image reminds you of, or what the image feels like, given the adjectives you just came up with. You can now go to the list of all the characters/objects in the dream, and write one or two adjectives next to each entity. You have begun the process of opening up to the meanings of the image via your adjectives.

Here are a few objects and people from my dream, "The Sun is Dying," along with a few adjectives about each one:

- The tower: tall, high, great view

- The books and papers: knowledge, information, big mess

- The farmer: close to earth, great self-effort, calm

- The blue light: light of spirit, emanates from Earth's atmosphere, color of sky (not regular daylight) that now illuminates my spiritual and worldly path.

By simply looking at the associations to each image, the dream meaning starts to emerge for me. After leaving the high perspective of the tower and the light itself changing from daylight to blue spiritual light, all situations occurring in my life are now being held in this wider context of my spiritual journey. The remaining characters and events will tell the rest of the story.

Dream Incubation

As you sit in bed at night with your dream journal, contemplate an issue, event, situation, or feeling in your life that you could use help with. Write a note to the "one who sends up the dreams," the "Dream Maker." Ask for a dream that will shed light on your chosen issue. In the morning, write out whatever came and embrace it with full certainty that the dream will give the help you asked for. Then do your dreamwork.

There are innumerable questions you can ask your Dream Maker: How can I improve my meditation practices? How can I handle the difficult communication with my friend? What is the best direction for me to go in my current work situation? How can I best prepare myself for the aging process? What will make me happiest right now in my daily life? How can I continue to develop compassion for all the pain existing for so many in today's world? What is the next best thing to do about?

Athena's Shield

CHAPTER 8:
DEEP DREAMWORK: LET THEM SPEAK

What follows is a process of role playing that allows the images to speak. Why create a process of role playing that allows the images to speak? In inviting the dream entities to speak, you avoid having the dream ego perspective be the only point of view put forth. In addition, you are allowing the multiplicity that is within you to have full voice. Everyone, all aspects of you, gets the microphone. By yourself, speaking out loud, writing in your journal, or with a good friend listening to you, become one of the dream entities.

Step into Dream Tadasana, the Basic Stance

The phrase, "I am" is a basic stance to take to align your energies with the dream image. *Tadasana,* or mountain pose, in Hatha Yoga practice is where the practitioners plant their feet on the ground as their body stands firm. When, in daily life, we say, "I am a woman, I am a doctor, I am a father," we are identifying for ourselves and others parts of our self that we have energy and meaning invested in. When we identify with dream images and say, "I am the snake, eagle, gypsy, apple, ocean, ..." we similarly stand in their energy and meaning. Standing in it allows the dream energy to flow through us and to do its healing or enlightening work. This is the dream tadasana, the basic stance to take when having dream images speak.

How Do You Become a Dream Entity?

- See yourself playing this dream entity as a role in a movie, dressed as this entity, or physically looking like it; i.e., "I am a gypsy, and have multicolored skirts on and a wild haircut," etc. Believe you actually know why you, as this entity, are in this dream, know what you are doing; i.e., "I have a very important message for this dreamer."

- Step into this entity by declaring that you are now "it." whether you get it or not! Keep in mind this is all a creative experiment; i.e., "Ok. I'm it. I am opening my mouth and I say...".

- Then say what you know, by allowing the dream entity to speak through you. You might not know exactly what to do or say right away, but do it anyway. Make it up. Just spontaneously open your mouth and talk, or, if you prefer, spontaneously write the statements in your journal. You will describe yourself, speak your thoughts and emotions, say what you are doing in the dream, say what you want the dreamer to know, etc.

- To get yourself going, you can start with, "Hello, I am the bridge/apple/child," etc. For example, here is what I say. "I am the gypsy and you had better come with me! I am very colorful and ready to go on some colorful adventures!"

Work with Dream Entities in Conflict

People often do not get along in daily life: witness the evening news and your family supper table to verify this. We also commonly find dream inhabitants that have conflicts and issues with each other. By looking at such conflicts, we unearth the troublesome issues we have occurring within ourselves, keeping us sleepless at night, or irritated with ourselves and others. What follows is an example of two dream entities that have a conflict.

A Dream Fragment from "Sun is Dying"

A wanderer walks into Paris and finds the huge stone castle where a woman is being kept prisoner. His mission is to rescue her. He enters the castle undetected by the untrustworthy man who owns it and finds the woman sleeping in a room at the top of the building.

Through the dream tadasana, the "I am" method, I become the untrustworthy man and the imprisoned woman. I allow them to speak to one another either written as dialogue in my dream journal, or I speak both of their parts out loud. If I speak out loud, I go back and forth, questioning the dream person, being the dream person and answering, and going back to the question-asking stance. Logistically, it helps to move from one side to another in your chair, one side for each character. In this way you get a bit of support in experiencing them as separate from each other; i.e., tip to the left and talk, tip to the right and talk.

MAN: The rich furnishings and great art in this castle are precious to me. I have it and you in safekeeping. No harm can come to you in here. I am your protector not your jail keeper.

IMPRISONED WOMAN: You have locked me in here, drugged and asleep. I hardly know where I am or what is going on in this world. What about my lost life in Paris, this wonderful city of love, art, and intimacy? I am denied so much by you.

MAN: You just accepted these conditions without saying anything. How was I to know?

WOMAN: You had your own agenda, your own plans. You never once thought of me as a real person. I have been caught in these dreams for a long time. And now I come awake. I see that an endless stream of color and energy pours through me. I am waking up and coming back to life.

To be continued....

I touch into the conflict between the two images just a little. There is no need to push it towards a false conclusion or jam the characters into false agreement. Honor the process where it is and let it simmer. There is much more here to uncover regarding the masculine energy that holds great power but keeps her imprisoned as a "sleeping beauty" woman, awakening to creativity and color. All of this is a work in progress.

Suggested Questions to Ask Dream Inhabitants

You can use any of the following questions in your dream dialogues with the various entities.

- Who are you and what are you doing in this dream?
- Describe your physical appearance in detail.
- What is it like being you in this dream?
- What activity are you involved in?
- Do you have a particular message for me, the dreamer?
- Do you have anything to say to anyone else in this dream scene?

If you are an object/location/building/ weather, nature objects, describe yourself.

- Who made you?
- What shape are you in?
- What are you made of?

- What is your purpose in this dream?

- What feeling do you embody?

- What do you say to the dreamer?

And, of course, make up your own questions as you move along in the conversation.

Tree Gazing

CHAPTER 9:
WEAVING DREAMWORK INTO LIFE

An important part of dreamwork involves honoring the messages and special images of the dream by weaving them into waking life as inspired actions and new explorations. What then happens when dream-based actions are woven into daily life? A surprising set of explorations, learnings, and suggested actions can present themselves.

Basically, via your dreamwork, you have walked into the labyrinth of the inner kingdom and come out bearing the treasure of a special image or message, which you then plant in these outer realms.

What follows are details and examples of how to do the weaving.

DREAM: THE NEWLY CROPPED BONSAI PLANT

I frequently visit a bonsai plant growing in a lovely park overlooking a scintillating blue harbor. (A bonsai, as you may know, is a tree or plant dwarfed and trained to grow in a certain design by special trimming and is a favorite of Japanese gardeners). I love being in the green company of this special plant. When I arrive on a particular day, I see that it is very dry and has been severely cropped; only a small stump of the original plant remains. I sit beside it and weep inconsolably.

The Bonsai in Waking Life

Here then is a collection of incidents and experiences with bonsai that simply happened without my seeking them out. In all of the experiences, various facets of the bonsai and her teachings are revealed to me.

- I have a small bonsai in my place of worship, which I attend to and water regularly. I feel the devotion of this small, repeated act green my heart.

- I notice my skin is as dry as that cropped bonsai. I start putting body cream on very frequently. Here is more devotion—this time to myself.

- I converse with a friend about the aging process and read a book by Jungian analyst Helen Luke on aging. How it is to face slowing down, seeing the gifts in it. I feel a bit like the cropped plant adjusting to a new, slightly more limited form. There is relief in this honest inquiry, and a subtle inner adjustment and harmony occurs.

- I do my spiritual practices one morning and appreciate the training I have received that allows me to embrace a daily discipline. The bonsai is like a student of the spiritual path, a living plant-in-training whose growth is directed in certain ways. I feel my own strength, commitment and discipline and also the way the hand of grace has formed me.

- An artist friend sketches the park, harbor, and bonsai for me. What a direct experience of birthing the living bonsai into this world! I am glad to lovingly share my vulnerable little bonsai with another person.

- I give a beloved teacher a beautiful, abundantly growing bonsai for a holiday gift. It is as though I harvested the dream and am giving a part of myself to the person. I feel the love that goes along with the gift.

- I attend an exhibit in NYC entitled "Van Gogh and the Colors of the Night." There is an exquisite painting called "The Sower" of a man sowing seeds in twilight. Beside him is a stunning cropped tree, with a handful of small, new branches growing out of the top. I have tears in my eyes and a tender feeling in the heart. How beautiful is the cropped tree, with its new growth and subtle Japanese expression. It so reminds me of my cropped Japanese bonsai. This time the tears are of joy in recognizing the delicate new growth. I have happily come back full circle to my dream park, my companionship with and grieving over that cropped tree, and I can now see it in a brand-new light.

You can see that the magical influence of the bonsai flowed on its own through my daily life. It had its own journey, and as it moved, revealed so many thoughts, feelings, and inner qualities. The key to this kind of image growing is love—loving the image that is your own inner artistic creation and knowing it is designed to speak to your heart.

DREAM: LAVENDER WATERS

A waterfall of mysterious lavender water sprays up unpredictably out of the earth in the middle of a busy mountain town. The lavender water is very soft, refined, reminiscent of clothing worn by religious orders, and seems holy or transformative in nature. It is a baptism for the whole town, although not everyone can see this. As the water pours down and spreads everywhere, I can observer sea people and sea horses riding the waves.

Lavender in Waking Life

- I behold the lavender waters flow gently around me in my daily life. Purple light continues to appear and dissolve in my meditation practice. It seems to create a soft, holy inner atmosphere. I am continuously soothed by it. My painting palette often lands on the cool violet-blue colors. It has a particular feel to it, a sense of rightness.

- I write a poem expressing how I am being led into the beautiful lavender forest of my own mind. That thought gives me the awareness that I can and do create beauty with my mind in my world.

- I purchase these delicious Prismacolor pens. One is called Imperial Violet, and I love the vivid lines it creates.

- I attend a meditation weekend the day after this dream, along with a large group of people. I experienced a baptism in the indrawn experience; in the true meaning of this ceremony, I felt welcomed into the meditation community through chanting.

- A while ago, someone gave me lavender perfume as a gift. The flowers are often dried and used in sachets as a pleasant scent. Herbalists say that lavender has healing properties and the ability to soothe, reduce inflammation, and is an aid to sleep. Lavender, if put under your pillow at night, is also said to enhance dream recall.

- Recently while repairing his house, a new neighbor cut down three huge, healthy, magnificent trees. He felt they were too close to his home, and he feared they would fall onto the house. I felt deeply upset by this event. While I made my peace with the neighbor, I felt like a close friend sat dismembered in my back yard. Early in the morning, I went with my lavender oils and its healing properties and rubbed some on each of the tree stumps and broken limbs. I held to the faith that this small act of lavender would help all the disrupted trees in the back yard. I felt soothed.

Honor the Dream in the Waking World

Dreamwork is a series of pretty interesting techniques or procedures designed to lead you to understanding your dreams. But it would be quite limiting and short-sighted to just do a process and extract an answer in order to merely improve your waking state.

Go back to the friendship you are now building with your dreaming life. You could wonder about and appreciate who or what is creating and sending these dream creatures up to you for your education. You can notice the tremendous creativity that flows from you even without your conscious awareness. Look how your so-called active imagination births many entities, some of whom become your lifelong friends.

Love and affection are generated, just as there might be in a relationship with another person in body. These dream creatures come to conscious awareness bearing great gifts and the experience that someone or something deep within has our very best interests at heart. Even if the dream entity is scary looking or monstrous in some way, we find out that it still has our best interests at heart in trying to get us to look at something and become more conscious. You can return again and again for conversation, advice, and guidance from these dream/imagination people.

Now it is time to invite your mind and intellect back into the process of dreamwork. First, what thoughts do you now have about your dreamwork? How does it illuminate your current life? Your past experiences?

Second, do some research. Look up information about your images, and generate a fascinating rich background for them. In doing research for my bonsai, I visited a place in Florida where there are many bonsai on display. I read materials on self-compassion and how Quan Yin is related to that divine virtue. I research any number of my other personal images, such as gypsies, oceans, temples, and eagles.

I fully enjoy dipping into the rich traditions of philosophies, cultures, and religions that include these symbols. These activities enrich the dreamwork adventure and generate inspired sharing with others who love their dreams.

Red Lighthouse

CHAPTER 10:
CONVERSATIONS WITH NATURE

Earth as Our Home

Earth is our Mother, no doubt about it. We are made from Earth's elements, nurtured by food growing in her soil, place our feet on her every day, live our lives directed by her cycles and seasons, breathe her air, and ultimately dissolve back into her when our Spirit leaves the body.

Yet there is a common, disturbing, and destructive relationship many people have with nature. In this relationship, we see and feel ourselves to be separate, even isolated, from nature's workings—impacted by it but not involved personally.

Yes, we experience nature and her mountains, oceans, trees, a myriad of growing things in her soil as something for us to delight in and rely on for inspiration.

But nature is also something to harness like a wild horse, or so we think. Even something to be frightened of, such as freezing winters with Arctic blasts, bringing sky-high heating bills. Something we wish to avoid, such as hurricanes with human names. Something to take in hand and conquer, as we find new places in the ocean and lands to extract oil from. Something to use, such as earth for crops and animals for food. Something to exploit, such as endlessly cutting down trees, or killing wild animals like elephants to then sell their tusks. Finally, nature is something we wish to scientifically understand, even after all the damage we as people have done to her.

In this time we live in, there is ongoing and dangerous confusion about what is truth and what is fiction, and therefore what appropriate action to take individually and as nations to handle these ever-increasing problems. There is the horrific impact of global warming not universally accepted as fact, and fires that destroy large tracts of land and homes. There are storms increasing in ferocity and our very lives threatened by virus and all of its offshoots, which continue to travel around the world at breakneck speed.

The creatures we share the Earth with have become second-class citizens, their habitats destroyed, some driven to destruction or extinction, all by our lack of true concern and sense of brotherhood for their well-being. Such devastation on Earth's shores, waters, fields, and skies is wrought by our own woundedness, trauma, and dangerously narrow personal and cultural perspectives.

Ignoring the tremendous damage that is being caused by our refusal to change our approach to Earth, coupled with this dangerously destructive relationship with Earth has an impact on our very souls.

Peter London is an artist, writer, and teacher with whom I have studied over the years, and I have watched my own heart turn forest-green in his presence. His teaching, writing, and art-making is married to being closer to nature and showing others how to do the same.

In his book, *Drawing Closer to Nature: Making Art in Dialogue with the Natural World*, Peter says of our current relationship with Earth: "Our culture's profound separation of humans from the rest of creation has produced a deep, diffuse, pervasive loneliness, disorientation, sense of loss, and fragility that is played out in all our relationships and through all our means of expression."

Being cut off from our authentic selves on the interior and also feeling isolation as a member of Earth's family creates, as Peter said, a sense of wandering, restlessness, and homelessness. And as we disrespect each other for whatever the reasons, the danger deepens.

Earth once said to me through a spontaneously written poem in my journal: "Without our heart-to-heart talks, you act like an orphaned child with dirty face and torn clothes wandering the streets crying for your mother."

My personal life is deeply impacted by what I see in my own backyard and neighborhood. A dog tied out to a tree for endless hours, his food thrown to him out the window by uncaring owners. The talk of the felled trees in my backyard cut down thoughtlessly by a neighbor wanting a better view from out his windows. The family of deer wandering in my neighborhood streets in early morning. So few birds eating at my feeders, while millions are found inexplicably dead, victims of global warming and smoke from forest fires released in the global atmosphere.

And, in Peter London's words, the degree to which we can "heal this broken primal relationship, our lives—mind, body, and spirit" could "take on a harmony, a grace, a wholeness, and an endlessly resourceful, gentle, and indomitable power."

We Nurture Each Other

Can we return to a profound and nurturing connection with Earth, once held by our early ancestors living on this land, and longed for by the people today who love this planet? We must entertain some new assumptions and perceptions about the true nature of Earth as she appears both in our waking and dreaming experience.

The Earth is a Conscious Being

Great beings and teachers say that this scintillating, sizzling-with-life planet is God embodied in the form of nature with all her phases, seasons, and lovely growing and living things. There is heart-stopping, staggering beauty in Earth's waters, mountains, trees, ice fields, desert sands, endless varieties of trees, flowers, flying and walking creatures, seasons and cycles, rainbows and rainstorms.

When seeing all of her moods, weather, season changes, and light, it is not hard to imagine her as being made of the highest consciousness. Soulfully and with our senses wide open, approach Earth as a fully alive being. Embrace her ability to grow things out of her magic soil, communicate in any number of ways, and bring healing to herself and us. These next stories, experiences, and dreams are examples of how to cultivate such a perception.

The Eyes of the Tree

I have loved and befriended trees at every age and stage of my life. The cherished relationship with the apple tree I sat in as an elementary school student; the tree my friend Harriet and I played in when we imagined we were living in Africa; a fir tree by a lake, which I sat under in my early 20s—I always had a special tree friend. There are many recent books about communications between trees in the forest and how they support each other in the face of threats from insects or other dangerous critters out to eat, chew, or otherwise do injury to them. Surely they all surround us with wise old energy.

During a visit to a retreat site in India, I am sitting on a stone wall in the vivid green gardens, drawing in my notebook in the noonday sun. I look up, see a tree, and see tree eyes looking back at me, fully alive and expressive. I rub my eyes hard. Perhaps I didn't see correctly. No, the tree is still there looking at me. I'm not tired, not asleep, not meditating, not lost in my own imagination. I even go inside a building and come back out again. It is still there, still looking. The tree spirit is alive, in the tree, looking at me, and I at him. For years I have read and studied the teaching that every form in this universe is filled with the same conscious energy. Am I being given a powerful example of this teaching that nature is fully alive and aware? I say "yes." Perhaps my love of trees drew this experience to me. My heart opened, and I felt in such loving companionship with this tree.

The Eagle is Alive

As a devotee of the Native American way and eagles for many years, I delved into the history and stories of the tribes who honored the eagle. At that time, I came into the possession of several eagle feathers, which I still cherish and honor. Further, I often visit the nearby lakeside Eagle Watch, especially in the spring, and check in on the eagles' nest and the young ones when they practice flying.

One day, I draw, then paint, an eagle from a photograph. In the middle of the process, something quite shocking and wonderful occurs. I feel the great bird on the other side of the canvas, pushing to come through, wanting to and making great efforts to arrive on the canvas. It becomes a presence joining me fully in the room, speaking to me, looking at me. I don't see how this is happening, but take my word for it, it is. He is fully present, and so remains till this day in the completed canvas. I recalled at that time studying about animal and bird totems choosing their people. Is that what happened? Maybe. Yet again, there is a powerful form coming alive, being conscious, in a completely unexpected way. Nature's mystery and presence responding to my love and devotion? I think so.

Nature Nourishes

When the senses are fully tuned, hear the blue jay in the back yard, see the squirrels dash up and down the trees, touch the pine needles on the tree adjoining your property in the forest, smell the roses in the front yard, feel a part of the sky while doing QiGong in the morning. Feed the snow birds, blue jays, cardinals, doves and woodpeckers, especially in winter. Wonder at the blankets of snow in the Northeast during midwinter, shovel the snow, and knock the icicles down. Mow the grass in summer and rake the autumn leaves. Water a geranium in your windowsill. Bring your loving awareness to these simple acts.

With your lovingly active imagination, befriend a tree by sitting with it at different times of the day and in various kinds of weather. While in a meditative space, notice any subtle energy, feelings, or body sensations flowing from the tree into your field of perception while in its presence. Perhaps the tree looks at you or speaks to you.

Repeat this as often as you can, and notice the friendship you are developing with the tree. Also research your chosen tree, and learn of its history and qualities. Does it enrich your newly forming relationship? Why this tree? Have you had a relationship with this or other trees before this assignment? What draws you to it?

Touch the tree trunk, notice its feel, and if you are so inclined, make some sketches of the bark. In imagination, have a conversation with the tree spirit that lives in your tree. What do you learn? See? Hear? Create this practice with joy and according to your individual inclinations. Plant trees yourself in your own yard and if you wish, all over the world via (Google it) "Team Trees."

Sit on a beach near the ocean waves and hear the continuous sound, its "breath" so like our own. Take in the seagull's cry, the wind off the waters, the magnificent sunrise. Pick up plastic bags from the sandy shores. Plant gardens and pick tomatoes; plant and enjoy spring flowers; work even in a small fashion with house plants. Clean up a stream with your neighbors; gaze at and paint a supreme sunset; grow your own wheatgrass; or turn your house green.

If we hold awareness with these ordinary, daily events, we become vessels open to receive the energy Earth has to give. We are plugged in to nature's energy like an electric cord into its socket. Then there is less of a sense of separation—replaced imperceptibly by a growing awareness of our inherent unity with all things. She is us; we are she. And the utmost honor, concern, and care can then be given to her in all her forms.

Earth as Supreme Teacher

We as her students can ask nature questions and look for her answers. Whenever I am near the ocean, I offer questions to her by writing them on the wet beach sands early in the morning. As well, I offer flowers to the ocean waves as they roll into shore. As the waves come in to wash my words away, and the little flowers tuck themselves into the shoreline rocks, it seemed that nature-as-ocean receives my communication. Once a seagull caught the little red flower I was tossing into the waves and flew around joyfully with the flower in his beak! I was thrilled. As I wait quietly on the shore or walk along the incoming tide, her answers often float up into my awareness.

Painting in the Mist

Once I held an art class on a misty evening, rain softly falling. As I sat in the outdoor pavilion waiting for the students to arrive, I was wrapped in a soft, mysterious atmosphere. In my little island of visibility, I could see the benches, parts of the walls, and the floor of the structure I was in. The trees, road, and art studio in the distance were shrouded in fog. Everything was soft around the edges and the mist, moved gently by a slight breeze, touched my face and hands, almost like foggy arms holding me in the moment.

The painting assignment that evening was to let the mist enter our being, as I had. We imbibed it through our skin and became it as we would a dream image. Its magic then came through our arms and hands onto the canvas or paper. What a way to dance gently with Mother Nature. Also came questions, "How am I 'mist' in my life?" "What do I make obscure or hide?"

A Dangerous Drive in the Snow

I was driving on a road through the mountains on the way to an art retreat in early winter. This road was famous for its steep turns and spectacular mountain views. As the squall of a coming snowstorm set in, I knew it could be exceedingly dangerous to drive.

Soon I noticed that my vision extended only into a small area in front of me and that everything else was whited out by the snow and fog. I could clearly see the road right in front and a bit to the sides, but no further. I moved between extreme fear and intense focus on the present moment, where I could actually see what I needed in order to continue driving.

I was also aware that this spectacularly lovely forest landscape had transformed into a scary, threatening place. This was a stern reminder to stay anchored in the present moment and in the body for there, and there alone, was the support I needed. There was the teaching.

Geese Honking in the Morning Fog

I stand in a four-story, castle-like building in the forest, a popular venue for visitors in a nearby retreat center. As I look out of the balcony windows, the mountains and the nearby forest are covered with morning mist. Concealed, but now out of the soft gray space, come three geese, flying by so close to me that I can hear their crisp wing feathers snap and their conversational, joyous morning honking. The air is scintillating, individual particles seem filled with life. I feel a strong sense of belonging and unity with the geese, mountains, trees, mist, and ensuing sunshine, thoroughly myself in all my shining aspects and creative expressions.

DREAM: THE OCEAN IS IN CHARGE

In a dream, I am driving on a highway towards a small island. The ocean to my left comes in and covers the road. Now I lose control of the steering as the wheels are no longer on the ground. I am so scared but have to do something, so I keep steering the wheel, even though the car is no longer being moved by my steering. In the dreamwork, the ocean speaks: "I am a powerful natural force, and when I take over, you are no longer steering. I take you to a place where I want you to be. Just let go. Be renewed in me, and have faith that I know what I'm doing.

Here is a tremendous teaching: let go, drop control, stay aware of higher powers moving me, and cooperate. Let go of clutching a wheel of my life, and see where I end up. In the language of the *I Ching*, let the Sage be in charge.

The Psyche Myth and Nature as Teacher

Some say that myth is actually a compilation of dreams held and re-dreamed over and over by a particular culture. What follows is a portion of the famous and well-told myth of Psyche and Amor, a tale of women's journey of individuation. In all of the four tasks given to Psyche by Aphrodite, her teacher, is the voice and hand of nature speaking in her many different forms. Here is the first task and what then happened to our heroine.

Beautiful Psyche, based on her promise to him to never look at his face, happily marries a wonderful man. In fact, he was the God of love, the son of Aphrodite. When Psyche couldn't resist, broke the agreement, and looked at him, she saw that he was really a God. He, according to his promise, flew away. She was then catapulted into her individuation process, a journey fraught with great challenge and several tasks given to her by her seemingly harsh teacher and mother-in-law, Aphrodite.

The first task was to sort out by the next day a huge pile of seeds dumped in front of her. "No way, cannot be done," she thought. This (and the future tasks given to her) were huge, insurmountable, and downright impossible in her eyes. She threw herself on the ground, wept, and threatened to end her life. Her personal effort alone would not be anywhere near enough to accomplish the job.

Thank Gods, while she slept (and maybe dreamed), an army of ants came and did the sorting of the seeds into nice neat piles. It is no surprise that the first task has to do with sorting. How many things have needed sorting in our spiritual or life journey? Family? Emotions? Intentions? Future plans? Our spiritual path?

When Psyche woke up the next morning, the job was complete. Unbelievable. What a surprise and unexpected relief to receive help like this. Help that came in the guise of one of nature's smallest and most clever creatures, the ants, creatures representing Pysche's hidden instinctual abilities. In the tasks that follow, it is also nature's creatures that again and again come to her help. The tall reeds growing by a large field instruct her on how to pull a small handful of golden fleece, representing male power, from the ferocious sheep grazing in the nearby field. An eagle takes a cup from her hand, fills it for her from a fast-moving mountain stream, and gives it back. She in turn gains the perspective and gaze of this high-flying creature. On the tale goes...Psyche in partnership with the natural forces in discovering her true nature.

We are Made of Awareness

Brian Swimme, a specialist in mathematical cosmology at the California Institute of Integral Studies, writes in story form his version of the beginning of the universe and our Earth. In his book *The Universe is a Green Dragon*, he makes a case for the view that we all do, and forever will, come from one source.

He says: "Our ancestry stretches back through the life forms and into the stars, back to the beginnings of the primeval fireball. This universe is a single multiform energetic unfolding of matter, mind, intelligence and life." This vivid description obviously includes us. We are actually bits of the stars, pieces of light, beings of awareness, now incarnated in human bodies, and can trace our beginnings back to this original primeval explosion.

This perspective invites us to practice unity vision, seeing all before us, including ourselves, as made from the same substance, the intelligent and loving light of awareness. It offers us a sublime view of ourselves—stars on the deepest levels and given our birth from nature herself.

Hafiz ecstatically captures this truth, as translated in the book *I Heard God Laughing*:

For the truth has been Divinely Conceived
Deeply within each of us.
O Hafiz,
Look at the Splendor of God's Grace:
The Sun has been planted in a thousand furrows
Across every soul's brow.

Amen, I say.

Becoming the Mountain, Lightning, Bear, and Waterfall

When you enter a dream scene and become a person or inanimate object like a car, you can, with active imagination, pull up associations, memories, thoughts, judgments, and you can speak as that object from your daily life activities and memories. As you do the dreamwork, you are psychically located in your own familiar language. In most cases you are identifying with a specific and familiar animate or inanimate object or entity.

But when you identify with and become something in nature, i.e., a mountain, a lightning storm, a roaring waterfall, a wolf, or polar bear, you are taking on the qualities of entities who are very powerful natural forces. They are impersonal. Let me spell it out: not related to human personality.

These untamed, elemental qualities and traits can move through you in a powerful healing or transforming manner. Witness the Native American people going into the mountains on a vision quest and meeting a totem animal whose energy and qualities they believe will guide them for life. Also honored are practices for imbibing the spirit of that animal. A friend and fellow therapist trained in Shamanic practices dances his totem, Black Bear, calling forth its energy when he has need for special healings with clients.

Now imagine becoming each of the four elements. You take on the qualities of air, its life-giving nature and constant movement. Air moving endlessly in and out of our very bodies, and with its exit, we too depart planet Earth. You become water with its ability to surround and flow through and by anything. Water, along with air, the foundational need that must be fulfilled to live on earth. You are earth, a magical substance out of which grows everything and with which all forms on this planet are formed. You are fire, the great consumer and giver of light. The fire in the body supports bodily processes, and the fire outside the body gives warmth and life.

Through them you sink into your own elemental nature, as you are basically woven from those four elements. Become space, or imagine that you are the sun, step into being the ocean, or a mountain.

John O'Donohue is an Irish poet and philosopher. Pat O'Donohue, his brother, said in the Foreword to John's book, *The Four Elements*, "As we journey from the womb of the sea with our gaze of longing fixed on the stars, we have stopped off on this Earth for a short spell of belonging. The unity of the four elements is what constitutes and sustains our existence in this world."

By recognizing the energy of these natural forces in your being, it is possible to extend and expand your own awareness beyond the workings of your mind and to move towards the experience of foundational unity of all things, which the great spiritual teachers speak of. All become a doorway to step into the invisible, expansive energy of consciousness.

With Love For Our Animals

What follows is a loving acknowledgment of the animals in the lives of my family, friends, dream lovers, and those dear ones supporting the creation of this book. With these beings walking, jumping, running, barking, flapping, and meowing beside us, we have far more love, joy, and delight in our lives. Not to mention that they are teachers who show us how to fully stand and play in the here and now. They are never second-class citizens to us but part of our family, deserving of every word of love and act of care, and appreciated for all they give.

For our precious Bennie the cat, joined by Duffy, Schaffie, Penny, Lulu, Dudley, Andri, Rosie, Giles, Dharma, Maxi, Bhakti, Jasmine, Kimball, Tucker, Callie, Bella Gray, Bruski, Kashi, Eddie, Murray, Charlie, Reggie, Maya, Nemo, Sunny, Blaze, Cecelia, Delphina, Dixie, Ginger, Cooper, Jack, Owl, Lily, Milo, Joey, Wicket, Ellie, Clover, Scampi, Maya, Peyton, Layla, Winnie, Coco, Story, Widget, Auri, Reizo, Trousers, Socks, Scruffy, Sam, Tigger, Chewy, Tom, Jerry, Reggie, Edwardo, Dexter, Oh Yeah, Ninja, Cosmo, Hazelnut, Blueberry, Purcy, Luna, Izzy, Tao, Gemma, Jupie, Cinco, Jay Jay, Mixa, Pumpkin, Gus, KG, and Country.

I also include the tigers whose photos I look at lovingly and with awe, the elephant whose image Larry wears around his neck, the 17-inch red-headed woodpecker who visits the suet holders in the winter, the owl seen and painted by my art mentor, the innumerable blue jays, snow birds, doves, and cardinals who arrive just now as we prepare for yet another Nor'easter snowstorm, and the black cat from across the street who is hiding under the porch making failed attempts to eat these birds. Last but not least, the red-winged blackbirds who thankfully herald spring. Thank you to one and all.

The Eagle

Chapter 11:
The Master Painter

Goings-on at the Top of the Turret: Revisiting the Big Dream

Big Dreams, such as "The Sun is Dying" described in chapter 1 of this book, are backdrops for one's whole life and can be looked at over and over throughout the years for new messages and guidance. Many years have passed since that dream and now, in a revisit to that dream, here is what emerged.

Dream

A man trudges on a dirt road to Paris to rescue a woman trapped in a huge stone castle. She is held by a very questionable castle guardian with seeming malicious intent.

The woman is discovered by this man in a room on a huge bed at the top of the castle. She bounces, twists, and turns while her body throws off huge streams of mysterious rainbow-colored material in all directions. She is rescued by this man who found her.

This stream of rainbow-colored material was surely an outpouring of my trapped and yet-to-be-expressed creative soul. This imprisoned dream woman contained aspects of my dormant creativity way back then, only to be discovered more fully in later years. In the Big Dream, the woman is awakened and, over time, set free in waking reality as an artist, writer, and an experiential teacher. All the colors of the artist's palette arise and come forth from her very body, splashing out onto future canvases, articles, books, or unusual teaching designs in workshops and classes. This dream encourages me to continue recognizing the artistic energy inside and to step free of any stone encasement I might dream up to limit myself. Then, I can take my delighted place on the artistic streets of Paris, my version of the art city of all times.

Painting the Canvas Miles

A fellow painter said that to claim yourself as an artist, you are required to paint several miles of canvas. Here is what happened when I worked on painting my miles.

The opening ceremonies for my painting process took place in a group I found myself in, designed for several artists to study their spiritual life through their drawings and paintings. I wondered from the outset, "Why am I here? And how am I here? I can hardly make any kind of artistic mark!" Someone in the group, later my art mentor, encouraged me to make strong marks on my paper without a lot of thought. Even then, I saw that something strong, though not necessarily identifiable, came out. There was something exhilarating about making those marks. I liked those images as much as I liked my dream images.

Over the next period of time, I worked out an agreement with a new friend in the art group who had kindly attended to me: I would teach him dreamwork, and he would teach me painting. It turns out that he was a loving and perceptive art mentor, and a talented artist himself. Having delved deeply into his own artistic soul, he knew how to focus not just on techniques but on the complex mental and emotional happenings inside the artists he taught that were apt to enhance or limit their painting process.

As I contemplatively looked inside regarding questions about my painting process for the very first time, I was shocked and delighted to see that my heart was filled with all the colors of the rainbow! Almost immediately after that inspired inner vision, I repetitively encountered a scramble of thoughts, feelings, uncertainties, and self-criticisms regarding my painting efforts. Okay. I would have to fight through this mental jungle to connect to that colorful heart.

I took a class in painting with Michele Casseau, the author of *Life, Paint, and Passion.* On her book cover, she wrote: "You are on your own, standing by yourself in the middle of creation. In the beauty of that aloneness, and in how you respond to it, you will find your passion." Wow. I was excited and uplifted. This class encouraged me to stand by myself, look inside, and paint what came up, with no editing, concern, judgment, or feedback from anyone including myself. Just pick up a brush, choose a color, and paint something. So I did.

Then, in my continued explorations, I took classes with Peter London, an inspired artist, teacher, and author of *Drawing Closer to Nature.* Peter said: "By drawing closer to Nature, we discover that we are nature. We were never, could never have been, exiled from our home." I was so touched by these words and deeply wanted the experience of being at home. So I tried painting outdoors, drawing mountains and trees and the sun. I lay on the grass and painted clouds, easy for someone with little drawing experience. I sat close to trees and rocks, feeling their textures and surface with my hands, and painted them. I took individual leaves inside, and at my desk, I drew them carefully. I drew sticks, twigs, leaves, tree bark, evergreen needles, all things small. I, as per Peter's suggestion, walked around, viewed, spoke to, and drew the tall and large stones living in earth for years—ancient entities with plenty to say. And then, trees, trees, and more trees.

I tried a class in a local school of art but became unbearably bored with ongoing assignments to perfect the drawing of squares or circles, or to embrace other lengthy art processes designed by the art teachers. I felt myself to be, well, impossible to deal with and full of conflicting needs: I did not know what I was doing or what I needed artistically. Yet I regularly kept choosing not to take help in a variety of forms but to wander off and unsuccessfully try to find my own way.

On, further on. I was afraid to draw buildings or people because I knew I didn't know how. I'm not saying this made sense. But it certainly showed how unwilling I was to step into the mystery and uncertainly of painting objects for the first time. My fingers seem glued to that table of familiarity. With this fear, I again saw how the mind and all of its judgments and odd shenanigans gets fully involved in the art process. Watching the mind? This art practice commands you to do that. Sometimes I painted from photographs or old nature calendars, then back to the outdoors when the seasons changed.

I continued art classes with my introspective mentor and, breathing a sigh of relief, I got back to noticing my own inner responses to the painting process. Over time and with ongoing effort, I grew to see I was following my heart regarding what I was choosing to paint. As these contented, comfortable feelings and a sense of rightness about my process grew a bit stronger, my mental aggravations and jumbled thinking grew smaller.

My love affair with images, always strong in dreamwork, continues to take on a new luster in the painting process. One never knows what the next dream might contain. In the same way, what are the next paintings that want to emerge from that inner mist or from richness of outer reality? For example, I enthusiastically welcomed the paintings of lighthouses included in this book. They are so meaningful to me as beacons of light.

A Second Big Dream: The Master Painter

In September 2013, I had a second most amazing Big Dream and a bookend to the earlier "The Sun is Dying" dream. This dream, entitled "The Master Painter," began a new phase of my painting process and the experience of Spirit operating in my dream and artistic life.

DREAM: THE MASTER PAINTER

I am in a wide hall like a warehouse with very high ceilings. On one side, from floor to ceiling, is a wall to paint on. In the room is a man. He is a short, dark-haired, wild, spontaneous person known as the Master Painter. He moves very quickly, and because of his speed, it is hard to actually see his face. He is the Master Painter, and this is his studio.

I am painting, completely absorbed and full of certainty as I put color and background on several huge canvases attached to the wall.

After this dream, I was awestruck. I immediately and enthusiastically turned to the process of recreating the paintings begun in the dream. The work, both in the dream, and then in the waking state, was done in a specific way. With no thought or plan, I lay out a colorful background with texture and moving lines, using as a starting point the colors of the dream canvases.

Images then simply appear or are subtly suggested in the background already laid out. Where they are coming from or where they are going remains a mystery until the painting is complete. I then select the images to focus upon and draw them out, slowly amplifying them, and allow them to grow and morph in ways that they seem to demand. For the first time, I experience painting with the power of Creative Spirit leading the way. This feels like an amazing experience of doing something and not being in any kind of control. Yes, a kind of non-doing, a release from identity with one's painting expectations and plans.

Forms that are only subtly present in the beginning become a bevy of goddesses and gods, as well as a whole host of mystical, magical animals, and enchanted scenes, all emanating simplicity, and a primitive, child-like quality. These forms capture the powerful processes of nature gods and goddesses or other invisible forces. I am deeply surprised and delighted.

I paint a particular space as both water and sky, another set of forms as both lion and hill god, and a cave maiden as an inner mountain range. The forms shift and move as the painting process continues. Here I am experiencing myself as the active, living, creator of that unusual God-populated world. I feel via my brush strokes that everything is made from the same exact substance: my paint! I also experience that the forms and elements can flexibly take on many different shapes simultaneously, expressing first one and then another form. All depending upon how I focus visually.

Spirit then emerges with profound observations of my painting process and questions for me. Can I transfer this felt experience as the creator of the painting to experiencing myself as the creator of my life? To truly get that I am creating my life in exactly the same way as I've made those paintings and that all in front of me in my life—trees, people, events, houses, cats, grocery stores, storms, birds, etc.—are also made of the same substance: consciousness, awareness. It is one thing to think or know this as true. It is another thing to experience and have faith in the truth.

Over time I have come to know that the Master Painter and the teachings offered in this painting process carry the touch, energy, and knowledge of my meditation teacher, Swami Muktananda, mentioned in the Introduction. Over and over, I have perceived his teachings of the unity of things: that all objects, living or not, are made from the same consciousness, as is my very life. And all that is created by us occurs via how we perceive and what meanings we bring to our seeing.

I concluded that the paintings, conceived deep within great archetypal spaces as described by Jung, arrived in my psyche, got cooked in my insides, and then took birth on the canvas. This way of painting seems a magical process straight from Spirit and certainly not under my control at all. And yes, the dreams, on a daily basis, arrive in pretty much the same way.

A year later these paintings were shown in my first exhibit called "Underground Dreaming" in Ruby Art Gallery, in upstate New York. As a delightful aside, Ruby Art Gallery was so named by a psychotherapist and fellow dream lover, who after a piece of dreamwork, decided that her true name was Ruby. She then labeled her adjoining office Ruby Art Gallery, where several exhibits were held over the next few years.

This event was lovingly supported by my husband who held my hand and hung the show, and my art mentor who guided my work on each of my canvases as they were painted. Present also was my dreamworker and therapist who, himself an artist, honored the exhibit by playing his flute during the proceedings. This is my favorite experience of being on the "streets of Paris" as a true artist.

Now I have gratefully accepted that both dreaming and painting, and as always, meditation, show me the way as I continue my spiritual journey.

In 2021, I find myself in deep meditation and moving in a colorful vision.

A MEDITATION VISION THAT SHOWS ME MY SPIRITUAL PATH

Bhagavan Nityananda, the teacher of my meditation teacher Swami Muktananda, is standing at the beginning of a path that wanders through the forest. He lifts his arm and motions to me, indicating that I should follow him.

He and I walk quickly up, up, on a steep path through the forest, through the rough hills, and stop on a high rocky cliff by the edge of the ocean. I join him, and together we look at an endless expanse of the mighty ocean as the waves roll in and as the stunning orange and yellow light brightens the sky.

When I wake up, I know that this scene is calling to be painted, so I do. In my painting imagination, Bhagavan Nityananda becomes a tall, red lighthouse, shining out on the ocean waves as the dawn arises in flashing orange color.

It has been my good fortune, as I have mentioned, to sit in the company of great teachers of meditation, to become deeply absorbed in yogic teachings, and to learn how to navigate the spiritual pathway.

I follow Bhagavan Nityananda, as I did in the dream, by studying his teachings. In these ongoing contemplations of his words, a treasured perspective emerges for me: to travel to my own heart, to live there, and to explore its pathways, mountains, valleys, and oceans thoroughly and joyfully.

Signposts of this great vision arise along the way in my travels both in dreaming and my waking life. In my waking life, I experience an ever-flourishing sense of compassion for myself and others, and a desire to see and act out of love. In the ongoing dreaming, my heart pours out color in the turret and then reveals a rainbow of color in my first painting contemplation. While these images do speak of my creativity, where else does creativity take place except in and from the heart? And now, having walked with Bhagavan Nityananda, I view the spectacular sunrise in my own heart. These three images are a cache of jewels that I receive from the dreams and lovingly hold.

I walk up the rough pathways while following the great teachings. I'm then invited to stand by the endless sea of events, looking out with a wide perspective at the brilliant color and beauty being shown in all things.

Coming Alive

PART II -
THE DREAM COMMUNITY SPEAKS

INTRODUCTION

When there was no six o'clock news
but just my voice on the inside,
thundering out dream visions for your daily
edification, you spoke "Dream Talk"
at breakfast with your neighbors and kids,
And then made your daily "to do" lists.

Judith Schafman

In various Native American tribes, people would wake up in the morning and regularly share dreams with family, friends, and the larger community. The dreams would dictate tribe activity for the day like hunting and planting. The Senoi, a Malaysian culture, were fully based on having integrated the dream and waking world. The Iroquois, according to Kaplan-William's research (see bibliography for information on both tribes), gathered annually for a dream sharing. In the Islamic culture, dream interpretation happened as a matter of course. In ancient Greece, for hundreds of years there existed dream temples. People would travel for many miles, rest, and receive healing dreams. The Bible itself has over seventy references to dreams and visions, thus encouraging people to see these phenomena as important and worthy of attention. Dreaming in many cultures over the ages, without fail, was considered the way that wisdom of Spirit would come into the tribe or family to deal with any number of issues or problems.

What follows in this chapter are dream stories from several committed dreamers who have found that wisdom pours into their lives through their dreams and dreamwork. I have worked on my own or their dreams with each of the contributors, and they also have worked with each other's dreams.

It is my wish that you too create friendships and community around your dream life. Nothing is as enriching and inspiring as having friends or family to share with. Make your dreamwork familial and tribal, and be sure to ask the children in your life what they have dreamed.

HAVIVA NER-DAVID: DREAMING IN SACRED WATERS

I am a rabbi and a spiritual companion with a specialty in dreamwork. I run a *mikveh*, a ritual immersion pool, in Galilee: Shmaya: A Mikveh for Mind, Body, and Soul. Water is my element, as I swim daily and feel most at home, at peace, and alive in water. I live with a degenerative genetic form of muscular dystrophy called FSHD, so it is only in water that I feel able to move freely and safely. It is not surprising, then, that mikveh and water have appeared in my dreams in various shapes and forms since I began paying attention.

Raised in an Orthodox Jewish home and close-knit religious community, I never fit in with the collective; nor did I find that the restrictive, highly structured lifestyle suited or was healthy for me. I longed for more freedom and rebelled against the system. At times, the side of me that longs for an illusion of control and wants to be accepted utilized the life structure as a way to ignore my deeper issues. My soul longed for meaning and connection, and Orthodox Judaism was the only way I knew to God. Despite my free spirit and universalist soul, I tried to contort myself to fit the religion of my childhood and play by that system's rules (both socially and religiously).

When I realized the toll this was taking on me emotionally and spiritually, I left Orthodoxy and called myself a post-denominational rabbi. But that feeling of constriction persisted. I began to question whether Judaism was the only place to find the answers I was seeking for my existential questions and struggle with my life and mortality.

Thus, I began deep inner work during four years studying at the One Spirit Interfaith-Interspiritual Seminary in New York, where I would address this persistent disquiet in my soul. It was in the One Spirit Program that I heard of dreamwork for the first time, and was deeply drawn to its workings and revelations. Here is the dream I had after first hearing of dreamwork.

DREAM

I am the officiating rabbi at a ceremony at Shmaya: A Mikveh for Mind, Body, and Soul. The ceremony involves the conversion of a baby to Judaism. When I approach the mikveh with the family, we realize there is no water in the mikveh. It has disappeared. I convince the family to come back after I refill the mikveh. But when we return, water is pouring out of the building: the windows, the door. It's flowing down the path, overflowing into and flooding the whole kibbutz. People are being lifted and carried away.

When I worked this dream, I spoke, according to the dreamwork principles I had learned, as the water. It became clear that I was expressing a need to return to my most essential, pure, core self—stripped away of layers of social conditioning and baggage—and return to overflow all constructed boundaries. When I spoke as the baby floating away, the child was moving away from being converted to Judaism. As this baby, I was able to let go of fear and calmly float away, trusting in the water to carry me where I needed to go spiritually, even if that meant breaking out of clear religious boundaries.

During the time I had this dream, my life partner, Jacob, was dealing with his father's deteriorating health. Jacob was spending almost half of his time in New York and half in Israel, so he could be with his father and help his mother and sister care for him. And since he had business there, too, he was able to be in both places.

That meant that I was single parenting our seven children for the time he was gone—with no family support system, since our families lived in the US. My own physical condition was deteriorating. I wanted to feel held, supported, taken care of, but there was no room for this or my spiritual longing in our lives. I had to bury them deeper inside me. Yet they refused to be silenced. They were knocking at the door of my dreamscape, calling out for attention. They were also expressing themselves in my religious unrest, that strong need for more room.

For example, a traditional Jewish Sabbath was feeling restrictive to me, so I had started driving on Shabbat (which is against traditional Jewish Sabbath observance norms) to swim in a heated pool about fifteen kilometers away, to explore natural, social, spiritual, and cultural activities in the area, and to generally expand my Shabbat horizons. Jacob was not comfortable with this, and it was creating friction in our relationship. Yet I was not willing to relent. I was feeling caged in, or like a kettle about to overflow. Then I had this dream:

DREAM

I am walking with my friend, who is on the kibbutz synagogue committee, on the way to services on Friday night. It was my turn to wash the synagogue floor this week. Now we are going there ahead of everyone else to set up. When we get to the synagogue, we see the building is in a cage with a bicycle lock on the front door. Water is streaming out of the windows, doors, and through the bars of the cage. The walls themselves are melting and flowing through the bars! "I guess I forgot to turn off the faucet," I say to my friend. "My mistake. I am so sorry." My friend says: "Mistake, huh?" winking at me.

I woke up with this powerful image. My unconscious knew what it was doing: erecting cages instead of fortresses to leave room for an eventual escape; leaving faucets on to keep the water running.

Creating flow where there was stagnancy, fluidity where there was solidity, merging where there was separation, and expanding overflow where there was containment.

Not long after I had this dream, I heard this "knock" from my unconscious in the form of a real-life experience.

I am walking to the mikveh with a group that has been on a spiritual tour of Israel, with their last stop—Shmaya. I have been emailing with the tour's guide for months to plan this meeting. The spiritual intensity and anticipation are high. Then I see the water flowing down the path leading out of the mikveh. My heart sinks. I had gone to the mikveh an hour before to set up. When the tour guide called to say they were running an hour late, I went home to wait. I remember turning on the faucet to let more water into the mikveh, but not turning it off!

I take a deep breath and close my eyes. But all is blank. I open them, and there is the group and the overflowing mikveh. This is not a dream. Or if it is, it is a dream seeping into my waking life. Something in my own energy created this intersection between my conscious and unconscious selves. Like my dream elements, my waking life was beginning to send me messages. The Universe in all of its unified energies, emerging patterns, and signs was speaking to me.

I forgot to close the faucet because I was distracted by life's events and demands. While I was setting up for the tour group, Jacob and I were discussing whether he should leave for the US ten days earlier than planned for his business trip, so that he could be with his parents. His father's condition had worsened, and his mother and sister requested that he come, for the third time in two months, to help them.

This did not come at a good time. I was still feeling emotionally and physically drained from his previous few trips. The kids and their needs were overwhelming me as I tried to understand the pain and neediness triggered in me, clearly the result of his frequent travel. Feelings of abandonment (by God, life, and my body) and overwhelm were flooding me like the mikveh waters were flooding the room. I had been feeling on the verge of tears for a good part of the past few months. I had been the one to turn on the faucet and then forget to turn it off. The unconscious has a way of making itself known.

Jacob's father passed. Jacob was still grieving and continued to travel between the US and Israel, but he was home more often, leaving space for us to attend to our relationship. With mutual appreciation and compassion, we found a place where we could both sit comfortably in our shared religious and spiritual life. I continued my spiritual seeking not confined to traditional Judaism, or even Judaism or organized religion. He opened his heart to my evolution, even as it challenged his assumptions about me and vision for our shared life. I had space to explore the depths of my existential suffering and begin to learn to surrender to the mystery.

That is when I had the following water dream:

DREAM

I am preparing to remarry Jacob in a second union renewal ceremony. It will be on the beach in Jaffa. But before the ceremony, a friend of mine who is studying to become a rabbi invites me to a women's group in preparation for the ceremony, in Jaffa's Old City. I am resistant because I do not usually go to gendered groups, but I go, and I am not sorry. It turns out that there are men there. Even Jacob is there. But it is being led by women, by feminine energy. This group will support me in attending this marriage renewal ceremony. I head down to the beach.

When I become the leader of this women's group, there is very strong energy present. I have the physical sensation that I am birthing myself into my own Truth. It is a profound experience. I feel myself drawing from a place deep within myself, my womb-like soul, like my waters are breaking and carrying me down to the sea, to remarry my beloved who, I discover, is me, Haviva, whose name means *Beloved*.

A couple of years later, I began having mikveh dreams again. Only this time, they were of a different kind. During the COVID-19 pandemic, I was involved in an effort to save a 2,000-year-old mikveh from destruction and have it transferred to our kibbutz beside the Shmaya mikveh.

On the day the mikveh was transferred to the kibbutz, however, I was at the hospital with Jacob, who had been diagnosed with a life-threatening, autoimmune skin disease. This was a frightening time made even more so by the fact that we were both now high risk for getting a bad case of the virus. While sitting at Jacob's hospital bedside, I was stunned to see an email from a dreamwork student, in which she shares her dream: *I am walking to my kibbutz to visit with Haviva and watch the ancient mikveh being delivered. A young man tells me Jacob and Haviva are not there; they had sailed away to an island to escape Israel's second wave of COVID-19.*

Given the intensity of my waking life during those past several weeks as well as the fact that my sleep had been fretful and interrupted, I had not been remembering my own dreams. It truly seemed my friend was dreaming for both of us. Her image of Jacob and me safe on a deserted island accompanied and comforted me during that difficult period, as I worried for our health. Whereas Jacob had always been the healthy one of the two of us, now we both had serious health issues. In fact, his were more pressing than mine. Which explains this dream I had a few days after the mikveh was transferred but waiting to be placed in the ground:

DREAM

I am standing at the site of the ancient and modern mikveh, which are now sitting side-by-side. We are trying to "re-plant" the ancient mikveh in its new home via a crane, but it is not fitting in the hole we dug for it. The engineer says, "This is literally like trying to fit a square peg into a round hole. Or is it a round peg into a square hole?"

When the ancient mikveh spoke, she told me that she could fit into the hole just fine if we removed the cage we had built around her in order to lift her and keep her from falling apart during the move. When I spoke from the voice of the engineer, continuing in his evocative and cryptic words, it became clear to me what this dream was about:

Jacob's and my relationship was continually evolving, deepening, shifting, and growing. Our roles within our partnership were becoming blurred—was he a square now and me a circle, or was I now a square and he a circle? Or perhaps we were now both squares and circles and would have to find a way to negotiate this complexity. The message of the dream was about taking on new paradigms and roles, about not trying to fit old ways into new circumstances—especially when not only was our reality shifting, but so were our positions and abilities and needs to give and receive within that changing reality.

What an amazing teacher my own dreamscape has proven to be. As Rabbi Hisda says in the *Babylonian Talmud: Tractate Berakoth* 55b: "A dream unexplored is like a letter not read." I feel open to whatever letters God sends in the form of dreams. Especially if the envelope is a mikveh!

Haviva Ner-David *is a rabbi and writer of both fiction and nonfiction. She is the founding rabbinic director of Shmaya: A Mikveh* *for Mind, Body, and Soul, where she officiates and creates water immersion ceremonies and does group workshops. A spiritual companion, Haviva practices sacred listening with individuals and couples and specializes in dreamwork. Her most recent book,* Dreaming Against the Current: A Rabbi's Soul Journey, *is a dream memoir. Haviva and her life partner, Jacob, live on Kibbutz Hannaton in Lower Galilee and have seven children, a dog, and a cat. Haviva lives with FSHD, a form of muscular dystrophy, which is one of her greatest teachers.*

TAMMY SATTERLEE: THE PRINCESS AND THE CASTLE

For many years, princesses and castles have been a theme in my life, both in outer world travels and in my own inner life. I have always had a fondness for anything that appeared royal and feel something captivating about the grandeur and uniqueness of a castle. In my life, I have traveled to castles all over the world. And the idea of being special enough to be a princess was a feeling that I longed to experience. I even named the location of my current home on the internet, "The Empress's Castle."

Recently an image of a castle and princess from my kindergarten years when I was a five-year-old keeps coming up. It is the same one that I used to ask the teacher's aide to draw for me. When I was recently teaching children in my own special education class, I made a miniature drawing or doodle of the princess and castle on a small piece of paper. Did she still look the same? Could I still draw her? When the image was drawn, I could not stop looking at it! I also noted that I did not put a face or an expression on the princess.

The home of Isabella Steward Gardner, which upon her death was made into a museum now named after her, is located in Boston, Massachusetts. It happens to be my favorite museum in the world. I first visited the museum while I was in college. During that visit, I purchased a postcard that I later framed, and it has been displayed in my home since. The image on the postcard is of a painting by John Singer Sargent. It is of Isabella dancing in a way that says, "I do not have a care in the world. I am fully myself." The painting is in the grand entrance of the museum.

My drawing of the castle and the princess reminds me of the home of Isabella Steward Gardner and that painting of Isabella dancing joyfully. However, my princess is expressionless, neutral.

I frequently have deeply reflected on my life as a five-year-old. At the time, my mother was suffering from serious mental health issues, my father had been diagnosed with cancer, and he was receiving chemo and radiation. I did not know or understand any of this, but in some way, I noticed the hushed conversations and the stress that was happening under our roof. My grandmother, Aunt Ruth, and Aunt Mary were often here tending to my sister and me. Many years later, as an inquiring adult, I learned that part of the reason they were here was because my mother was unable to care for us emotionally.

In working the "waking dream" of the princess in my drawing, I learned that she is a deep and most beautiful part of me and represents my higher, Divine Self. The exquisite castle where she is meant to live is filled with precious, beautiful, and ornate furniture, all built specifically for her. Yet, she had been separated from where she truly belongs, in the same way that I had been kept out of my own expressive, creative self as a child.

During those early childhood years, I was forced to "grow up" and set aside my true childlike needs, hopes, and desires. Instead, I kept to myself and retreated into a place that kept me from sharing the beauty and richness within. I kept those special parts hidden, even from myself. Judging by the princess's lack of expression, I was also hiding my emotion from the outside world, my expressionless face being whatever anyone else wanted it to be.

Caroline Myss's book and lecture, *Entering the Castle*, is based on Theresa of Avila and her book, *Interior Castle*. Her descriptions of finally entering "the castle" has great meaning for me as it involves stepping into the deepest part of oneself. I have been thinking a lot about the princess as located outside of the castle in the drawing. It is now fully time for her to step into the castle to become the queen!

In a recent letter to God (one of my regular spiritual practices is to write letters to God), I wrote: "This whole idea of stepping into the castle as The Queen is so exciting to me." I imagine having a celebration ritual for myself for becoming crowned "Queen."

The time I imagined a ceremony coincided with the time my daughter would be moving out of the house to go to college. I knew that my life was ready to shift in a major way.

Over the course of the next several days, I worked on cleaning out my basement. I am realizing that in cleaning out the "mansions" in my own home, as in the book *Entering the Castle*, I am preparing the way for God and Spirit to enter. I am finally beginning to understand the process of clearing out the "reptiles," as Theresa of Avila said, and doing as Henry Nowen teaches, "becoming the beloved."

I am thinking of Theresa talking about the monks sweeping the floor and the work I did cleaning out the attic, the garage, and now the basement. I too have been cleaning out the cobwebs of my Soul and trust that God will further show me the way.

When my cleaning was complete, my son Nathan helped me to take many things to the dump. That evening I had a modern-day celebration for finally entering my own castle and becoming its queen. I bought myself a NY steak and grilled it for dinner. I also made veggies, opened up a bottle of red wine, and had it with cheese and crackers as I was preparing my dinner. It was as if I had company present, but it was just me!

The castle and princess process has presented itself in a recent dream since then.

DREAM

Two women and I are walking toward a house that belonged to one of the women. It was a big mansion that I was planning to stay in with her. I also had some sense that it was going to be my new home.

However, when we got to her house, I realized up ahead there was an even bigger home that was going to be mine, and it was gorgeous. There were several men working on it, sanding beautiful, intricate pillars that were detailed with elaborate faces and designs in them. At first I was worried about them accidentally sanding something off, but I could see the man in charge was doing all the detail work.

He came down when he saw me and asked me a question, suggesting I had a husband who bought the house for me. I called back, "There is no husband." I felt proud of the fact that I spoke it as, "How dare you assume I didn't earn this on my own!" Then he got in his truck for some supplies, and I kept walking in awe that the beautiful home was mine.

I have arrived. I am home. Finally, the princess has been reunited with her castle and is its queen.

Tammy Satterlee *is a minister and spiritual counselor. She is a former Special Education teacher currently working with parents and children as a Family Engagement Coordinator in pursuit of becoming a licensed mental health therapist. "I guide people to discover their soul gifts and inner divinity through the practices of sacred ritual and ceremony, dream work, soul collage, creative art and spiritual practices." www.lovetammy.net*

SARA TUCKER: RIDING WAVES WITH OCEAN GODDESSES

DREAM

I am on a long journey through the grounds of a large estate, trying to leave a party where I no longer belong. After trailing through many gardens, I arrive at a shallow swimming pool, empty except for two black dogs that have been waiting for me. I am to teach them a way to play in the water—swirling my legs below the water while my body above water remains stationary—something I did with my younger sister when we were very young. The dogs immediately try to imitate my movements. I then question if the pool is deeper and move to find the deep end.

At the time of this dream, I was at a major turning point. My 60th birthday was approaching, my children were grown and establishing independent lives, and I had decided to retire from a 26-year career that I had wanted to leave for some time. Though I did not have a clear plan for what was next, I knew it was time to open myself up for something new to emerge.

My original plan to mark my late-November birthday was to travel to Galilee, Israel for a ritual immersion in a mikveh, a plan upended by the pandemic. Continuing to design an alternate plan for the ceremonial immersion, I considered a river, a swimming pool, the shower, the ocean. I settled on the ocean at a beach about two miles from my home. With each of the seven required immersions, I intended to step more fully into my power as a woman of sixty.

I had not been in the ocean near my home for over 20 years and had to confirm that I could tolerate the cold waves. I purchased my first wet suit and joined two friends who regularly boogie-boarded.

With them I spent the next two months, prior to my ritual, boogie boarding a few times a week. I found it enlivening and invigorating and laughed much more than I had in years as my friends and I rode the breaking waves!

With each visit to the ocean, I entered the water with reverence. I imagined the Yoruba Goddess of the Living Ocean, Yemaya, who presides over surface waters, rushing toward me. Once out in the water and riding toward shore, I looked to either side of me, seeing the Celtic goddess Rhiannon, a loving Welsh Goddess, riding her white mare in the bubbling water of the breaking waves.

As the ocean holds me, rushes all around and through me, I am somehow allowed to fuse with her energy. Her fierceness and beauty surround me, her laughter sounds in the crashing waves. There is also a graciousness and welcome I feel while being in the waters lovingly guided and directed by the Goddess. The process brings me closer to the life-giving power and beauty of nature than I had been in years.

I was nervous and excited as the day approached—so much thought and planning had gone into preparing for this powerful event. The dream of the swimming pool reassured me of the rightness of the process of transformation I was stepping into.

The dream path I took through the estate, to leave a gathering I no longer belonged in, and a version of myself I no longer was identified with, highlighted the journey to this special immersion in my waking life. In the dream I kept moving past various hurdles, ultimately alone as I approached the pool, just as I would be when I walked into the water on my birthday.

On the appointed day with the ocean, I took my time with each *kavana* (immersion). No rush. The sixth immersion was one of silence, listening. What I heard was "flow with it; float," a gentle urging to be with what is, in a light way. After all seven immersions, I decided to swirl around in the water like I had in my dream, and exactly as I did as a young girl, playing with my sister Liza in the swimming pool.

In this way, the dream not only reassured me, it also reminded me that the playful energies of my childhood self could co-exist with the deeper callings of my soul as I age. While the immersion itself was now over, throughout the experience of preparing for and going through it, I became closer to my own longing for an ecstatic connection with nature's earth, trees, sun, moon, animals, and growing things. It is my heart's desire to feel her full power, beauty, and mystery, much like I had felt with the ocean who had received me so graciously in my immersion experiences.

Footnote: The Yoruba people are originally from present-day Nigeria, Benin, and Togo.

Sara Tucker *is an ordained interfaith minister and spiritual counselor with an extensive background in mindfulness work and executive coaching. She delights in traditional Irish singing and is committed to her ministry of singing at the bedsides of people who are dying. She and her partner have raised three children, all now making their way in the world.*

KARA CHE BARTOW: THE RHINOCEROS

In September of 2021, as my medically-fragile 19-year-old stepson lay at home under hospice care, facing the end of his life, I had a dream that baffled me completely.

DREAM

I had learned of a rhinoceros at a nearby zoo that needed medical treatment to survive. I had never seen the animal but was very moved by its plight, so I dipped into my savings and gave every penny I had to help heal it. I sent thousands upon thousands of dollars to the zoo for the purpose of funding surgeries, medication, and anything else the rhinoceros might need to live.

I found myself driving a car at nighttime, following a large, enclosed tractor-trailer down a dark highway. I knew intuitively that the rhinoceros was inside the vehicle, and I was following along to make sure that he got to his new home safely. During the journey, I was in contact, via walkie-talkie, with the medical team that was caring for the rhino. They reassured me that he was recovering well from surgery and was stable and comfortable. I was relieved. I relaxed into knowing that he would live, and that he was well cared for.

Suddenly, the trailer stopped, and all of the lights on the truck went out. I could see the dark shape of the semi in front of me in the glow of my headlights, but there was no response from the walkie-talkie. I began to panic.

Every possible fear came to me: the truck broke down, and we are stuck out here in the dead of night; the rhinoceros took a turn for the worse and is dying; this whole thing was a hoax...they took my money and now they are going to come and kill me. Each fear scenario was worse than the last. But, suddenly the lights on the truck came back on, and I heard a voice from the walkie-talkie saying, "Sorry, we just had some vehicle trouble; it's all taken care of." I confirmed that the rhino was okay, and we began driving.

Despite my relief that we were moving again, I suddenly felt a heavy sadness wash over me. I was aware that, even when the rhino got to where it was going, I was not going to get the opportunity to meet it. I had given so much to this creature but would never know it or look into its eyes. In my dream, I cried for that feeling of loss.

This was the moment when I awoke, befuddled by the appearance of a rhinoceros in my dreams. I had never been much interested in rhinos or been drawn to them in any way. There are so many animals that I have felt an affinity for, but not the rhinoceros. Yet here was a very powerful dream that had gripped me and refused to be forgotten.

I brought the dream to some dear dreamer friends, women who have never let me down when it comes to supporting my investigation into my dreams.

In the course of talking with these women, I spoke for the rhino and described myself as "strong and gentle." I reported feeling safe and knowing that those caring for me were good, and I trusted them. I recognized that, as the rhino, I did not know where I was going, but that I trusted it was safe and it was the right place for me.

As I worked with the dream further, I realized that the moment of darkness mirrored my own fears as I watched my stepson's health decline. As his spirit moved closer to the unknown, I followed along, determined to ensure his gentle passage into his next adventure. Despite those moments of fear, I continued to follow him, to be with him on his journey. And I believed that he felt safe and loved by me. That he trusted me.

By this point, I was in tears. I remembered the dream-moment of sadness as I realized I would never get to know the rhinoceros. This too was a mirror of my life. My stepson attempted suicide at age 11, about three years before I met him. As a result, he suffered an anoxic brain injury that left him unable to move or speak. He was unable even to make facial expressions to communicate pleasure and distress.

My wife has shown me pictures of him before his injury and shared drawings and writings he did as a child. I've seen videos and heard stories about his big heart, his creativity, his abundance of love. Yet, I never got to experience him that way, and it pains me. It feels like a loss. And yet, as with the rhino, I chose to take on his care as a part of my life. That has meant days and nights (sometimes weeks) in the hospital. It has meant nurses in our home 10 hours/day and 10 hours overnight. It has meant providing his meals via a tube in his stomach, changing his soiled briefs, suctioning his tracheostomy, dressing him, using a lift to move him to his chair. In many moments, it has taken everything I have.

And still, in my dream, I was with him on his final journey, making sure he was safe and comfortable; making sure he felt loved and unafraid, even though I didn't know where he was going, and I couldn't go with him.

Several weeks after this dream, I had another very short dream.

DREAM

The rhinoceros came to me again. In this brief vision, a massive, larger-than-life lion was attacking an elephant. However, just as the lion sprung, the rhino charged in between the two animals and blocked the lion's attack. The rhino did not fight but effectively stopped the attack. It seemed to be made of an armor the lion's teeth and claws could not penetrate. It simply blocked the attack again and again, keeping the elephant safe.

When I discussed this dream with my dream friends, it became clear, again through tears of understanding, that the lion was not malicious. It was simply doing its job, fulfilling its purpose on the Earth. I recognized it less as death itself than as the pain of death. It was a predator, doing what predators do. Death is an ever-present reality of life and a part of nature.

The elephant was wise, calm, and kind. So, here was death, and the fear of death, attacking my wisdom, serenity, and basic goodness.

But the rhinoceros, simply by placing itself between opposing forces, gently said, "No." The rhinoceros—who symbolized gentle groundedness and a spiritual perspective on the cycle of life and death—was protecting my wisdom from fear of pain and death. Perhaps it was my own vision of my son, telling me not to be afraid of death, that he did not fear it and would not let it destroy his wisdom, nor did I need to let it destroy mine.

One of my dream friends during this time did some research on the rhinoceros and found a surprising and lovely gift, something I certainly never heard of, called *The Rhinoceros Sutra*. Reminding me of what both my son and myself were going through, it read: "Without resistance in all four directions, content with whatever you get, enduring troubles with no dismay, undisturbed at the ending of life, wander alone like a rhinoceros."

On October 27, 2021, my son died, surrounded by love. We held his hands and stroked his hair. We told him how much we loved him and all that he had given to us. We played music and sang to him. In our hearts and our minds, we held him in love until the time came for him to go.

This was the moment from my dream: I was in the car, following the rhino as he moved forward into a new adventure, another home, and that, while that future was unknown to me and to all of us surrounding him, he trusted in our care, and we could love him and guide him toward peace.

I am reminded to remember who it was that I was caring for. No fragile creature, my son. He was a giant, a strong and gentle being I had the privilege of knowing, caring for, and sharing a life and home with for many years. I was fortunate to be beside him to the end of his short life.

Kara Che Bartow *helps children to communicate as a speech-language pathologist specializing in pediatrics, with emphasis in the area of autism. In her free time, she draws, paints, takes photographs, and is writing a book about the adventures of five unique, unpredictable children. She enjoys spending time with her wife, son, and their six cats and dogs, three of each.*

ROB SANDUCCI, PHD: DREAMING WIDE AWAKE

There is a thin veil between waking and sleeping dreams. Perhaps... There are experiences that suggest there is no veil, no separation, at all. This notion is clearly supported by Eastern religions and quantum physics. Both speak of a "field" or invisible space out of which everything comes and in which everything exists. Further, there is a way in which many dreams, unhampered by our strong waking sense of past, present, and future, portend or even predict future events. The following waking and sleeping dreams reflect these notions.

DREAM: INITIATION

I am near Tivoli visiting a newly built monastery. I am invited to sit with a lama (looks like the Dalai Lama when he was about 40). He's alone in the meditation hall as I peer in through the door. He motions for me to come in and sit next him on a red zafu. He laughs and pats the zafu motioning for me to sit. We begin to meditate as we breathe in silence; I feel a blessing and a healing simply being in his presence.

As I approach the door to leave the hall I turn and bow. I then encounter a woman, who is also a Tibetan lama, in her forties with black hair and striking blue eyes—so clear. She tells me that everywhere she digs on this land, the area immediately fills with water, so she is planting water lilies, lotus flowers, and other tropical flowering water plants.

As she walks with me back to the entrance, she smiles and encourages me to return and visit soon. I slowly turn and as I am walking away, I become aware that I am wearing a red monk's robe and simple sandals. "How did this happen?" I think to myself. The robe seems to be a perfect fit, size, and length—as if it were tailored specifically for me. I walk slowly, as if in meditation, with a peaceful calm in my heart as I return to my home in Tivoli.

Commentary

Tivoli is a small hamlet situated on the Hudson River in upstate New York. Within a year of having this dream, a Tibetan monastery was constructed about five miles from my home, and I began seeing Tibetan monks in their robes and sandals in local stores and on the street.

DREAM: THE MONK

I am looking out on the pond where we live and noticing the mist above the water. Slowly the mist is rising into a form that looks like a Zen monk sitting in meditation. I walk to the edge of the water and realize the bald monk is Patrick. Then he looks directly at me and says, "Don't wait!!"

Commentary

Patrick is my wife's uncle whom we were very close to, especially at the time of this dream. He was in the hospital being treated for lung cancer and due to chemotherapy had lost all his hair. When I woke from the dream and went downstairs to make our morning tea, I noticed the message light on our phone was blinking. A relative had called to tell us Patrick died overnight.

When I thought of the message, "Don't wait," I took it to mean pursuing and completing my doctorate in psychology, increasing flute lessons, and buying a home.

Within a year and a half of this dream, all three occurred. So, it is important to not only plumb the meaning of a dream, but also ask, "What does this dream want me to do?"

DREAM: SURRENDER

I am driving my black Volvo on a familiar road near my house. It has snowed overnight with freezing rain. Even though I am driving slowly, the Volvo begins to skid out of control. Suddenly a spiritual teacher appears in her beautiful robe standing in the road, her hand raised symbolically to stop. The car comes to a halt right in front of her close enough to see the red *bindi* on her third eye.

Commentary

That very morning driving to the office in my black Volvo, I hit a patch of black ice. The car began skidding out of control. I remembered the dream teacher's posture and took my foot off the gas and let go of the steering wheel in a state of complete surrender. The car drifted as if in slow motion to the side of the road coming to a complete stop, inches from the guard rail.

DREAM: MY HUSBAND IS COMING

This brief dream vignette occurred in 1981 when my then-unmarried wife, Barbara, was living in New York City, and I was living in upstate New York. In her dream, she is told that she is going to marry a man named Rob. We met in 1987—a mythic waking dream story in and of itself!—and married in 2000.

WAKING DREAM: SYNCHRONICITY

I am in my therapist's waiting room 15 minutes before my scheduled session. Picking up a copy of *Yoga Journal,* I was captivated by a cover article and picture of Arnold Mindell, PhD, with the caption: "Dreambody Psychotherapy." I became quickly absorbed in the article/interview with Dr. Mindell who had just published his first book, *Dreambody: The Body's Role in Revealing the Self.* After the session I ran to the nearest newsstand to get a copy of *Yoga Journal* to finish reading the article. When I opened the magazine looking for it, I was stunned to discover that my therapist/supervisor, Bud Feder, PhD, had also contributed an article entitled "Yoga and Gestalt Psychotherapy."

Commentary

A little background information: At that time, I'd been in a supervision group with Bud for eight years and recently challenged the group to focus more on dreams and their relationship to the body. Although still working with Bud and the group, within two years I also began to study with Dr. Mindell, who at that time gave seminars through Omega Institute, NY. It was at the close of a pivotal weekend workshop that I learned Dr. Mindell would be offering an advanced training for therapists in Oregon and two weeks after, a seminar exploring addictions, held in Hawaii. Could I do both? A radical notion given limited funds and needing time off other clinical consulting responsibilities.

A decision, I knew, would not be able to be made solely from a pragmatic, rational, linear approach. So, I utilized a lucid dreaming technique to simply write a question to the "dream maker" to see what comes through. "Should I go to Portland or Hawaii?" The following is a response to my dream inquiry.

DREAM: WHEN THE STUDENT IS READY, THE TEACHER APPEARS.

Arny (Dr. Mindell) and I are leading a workshop together. A conflict erupts between two men. One man says he's too angry to continue so I encourage him to make angry sounds without words. He growls and eventually screams that he is angry at God. In the middle of this intense scene, Arny and I are ushered to a private room where we are served a special lunch of angel-hair pasta. Arny is encouraging me to get more involved in his Process/Dreambody seminars and become part of the teaching staff.

Commentary

In listening deeply to the dream and exploring the image of angel-hair pasta, I thought, "Of course, I'm Italian and love pasta." Yet why specifically angel hair? Knowing the dream-maker always selects images with a genius, I got it. Angel-hair pasta is spiritual food that I am sharing with Arny. Perhaps beyond being a brilliant physicist and psychologist, he might also become a spiritual teacher for me.

And so, I called my travel agent and booked flights to Portland *and* Honolulu.

In those early seminars, a mentoring relationship was fused that spanned more than a decade, including Arny agreeing to chair my doctoral committee and inviting me to assist him in workshops held in the Northeast.

Several years later, when I was assisting Arny at an Omega Institute workshop, he approached me after a lunch break to tell me during his nap he'd had a dream about me.

ARNY'S DREAM: SANDUCCI BOULEVARD

I wanted to talk with you, and someone told me you were in a building up the hill beyond this seminar hall. I walked to find you, yet couldn't get near the building because of a long line of people waiting to see you. Then I looked up and the road sign read: Sanducci Boulevard.

Commentary

The building Arny unknowingly pointed to was a Wellness Center on campus where I had been hired by Omega Institute to do dreambody consults with people suffering from different illnesses. Prior to Arny's dream, I would often have only two or three appointments. That very week my schedule became full—in excess of ten appointments with a waiting list—and remained so the rest of my tenure there.

In summary, all dreams are portending the future to some degree, and much like the sleeping/waking dreams I have shared, some dreams are literally predicting the future!

Rob Sanducci, PhD *is in private practice in Red Hook, NY, and specializes in clinical supervision, couples therapy, and treatment of psycho-physical illness and dreamwork.*

LARRY SCHAFMAN: WIN, PLACE, AND SHOW AT PIMLICO

I was at a major turning point in my life in the mid-1970s. I was coming up for a tenure vote at the community college outside of Baltimore where I had been teaching history since 1970. I had been living in a house in Baltimore with my partner of three years, who was head of the Psychology Department at the same college. My prospects for receiving tenure were diminishing by the day. I could not even think about next options for work. How would I feel as an unemployed history professor when the market for this kind of job was extremely limited? Would Judy and I stay in our rental house in Baltimore?

Around this time, Erhard Seminars Training (EST) was popular in the progressive Baltimore-Washington community. Friends had taken it, and they spoke about it changing their lives. Over two consecutive weekends, they learned about making agreements with themselves and taking full responsibility for their lives. It sounded pretty good to me as I was facing some tough decisions. Because I would not be earning anything but unemployment checks in the near future, I was worried about affording the $250 training fee.

It was early May, and the Preakness Horse Race was coming up on Saturday at nearby Baltimore's Pimlico Race Course. It was an exciting event and a big deal for the Baltimore community. On Tuesday before the race, in a very deep sleep I had an unusual dream.

DREAM

I am in a large building with many corridors and rooms. I'm looking for a particular room where I would attend a class. I try different doors, and some are locked. One that opens is not the right room. When I finally come to the right room, I find out that I need to pay for the class before I could go in. The fee is $250. I do not have that amount of money, so I leave the area and wander to another space that opens to the outside.

When I go outside, I see that I am at the Preakness, and the race is about to begin. I take a seat that is near the finish line. The horses go by for the first time and are all bunched closely together. Watching across the infield to the other side of the racing oval, three or four horses are together at the lead. They come around the far turn and are heading for home—the finish line. My eyes are glued on the group of four, and I see all their numbers. As they cross the line, Number 9 clearly wins. Number 5 is second. There was no way to tell which of the two other horses comes in the show position. It is definitely a photo finish. It is either going to be Number 6 or Number 15. Then, I woke up from the dream and wrote it down.

As fate would have it, that morning we were invited over to a colleague of Judy's in the Psychology Department to meet a special guest of hers. Dr. Ann Faraday was a very popular author of *Dream Power* that had helped more than 500,000 people recognize the importance of their dreams and learn how to use the messages and information they reveal to *enrich* (my emphasis) their lives.

During a very interesting discussion of dreams, I told Dr. Faraday about my Preakness dream. Immediately, she encouraged me to go to the race on Saturday and bet on the winning horse number. I loved the idea, but I would not be able to attend the Preakness. So, I decided to go to Pimlico the day before.

In the feature race of the day, the Black-Eyed-Susan Stakes, I went to the betting window. I placed two ten-dollar Trifecta bets on the first three horses to finish. One bet was 9-5-6 and the other was 9-5-15.

I went back to the finish line area to my seat, with the two tickets in my clutched fist. The race began. When the horses reached the far side of the track, I noticed that a group of four horses were close together out front, with the rest of the pack lagging behind. As they entered the backstretch, these four horses were fully separated from all the others and racing for the finish. As they crossed the line, I saw that Number 9 won, Number 5 placed, and the two other horses were neck and neck for third place. I could see Number 6 but the other horse was behind him, and I did not see the number. As I kept my eyes on them as they slowed up, I could read very clearly the number 15. I knew, unless there was an objection, that I had won one of the two bets!

The photo sign went on in the infield tote board. It took a few minutes before they posted the official results. Nine. Five. Fifteen. The winning Trifecta paid $250. That day I registered for the EST Training.

Larry Schafman *is a public relations consultant celebrating the achievements of children and staff at the Fallsburg, NY, Central School District with his photography and writing skills. His previous careers were as college history professor, general contractor, and building manager for a non-profit organization. He learned the importance of his dreams in psychotherapy and Jungian analysis in the early 1970s. At that time, he had the good fortune to meet Judy, the "girl of his dreams."*

FURTHER IN, HIGHER UP

British author C. S. Lewis evokes the clarion call for inner exploration. Through the voices of several animals and people in his book, *The Last Battle*, from the *Chronicles of Narnia*, he describes the power and pull of the inner worlds and calls to people to come:

> "Further in and higher up!"...
> "Come further in! Come further up," he shouted over his shoulder"...
> "Don't stop. Further up and further in. Take it in your stride"...
> "The further up and the further in you go, the bigger everything gets. The inside is larger than the outside."

Through dreamwork and the skillful spiritual practices of meditation, contemplation, artistic activity, along with a variety of psychological means, the inner journey can take you to the highest and deepest places of your own soul. Intend to discover what "further up" in your being means. Then find the way to see what "further in" means for you within your own heart and soul. You will expand the spaces of your own inner being by your choices, and you will delight in your learning. Time swiftly moves... Well?

Now what follows is my way of concluding our current adventures. Recalling the great snake with a blue tooth I described pages ago:

DREAM: BLUE SNAKE SITTING ON A BAR STOOL

I now meet another lively blue dream-snake with rainbow-colored stripes. He is sitting on a stool at a bar in front of me and is eager to talk.

I remember how Persian saint Hafiz writes poems often set in barrooms, where the wine of spirit and love flows freely. Hopefully, that is the bar I am in now.

So the snake and I talk in a fascinating dreamwork dialogue. I am sitting in my art studio in my own waking state and am now asking her various questions while I sketch her or him.

Ahhh. The snake tells me she is the voice of my own dreaming over these many years. She has penetrating statements to make about what all of this dreamwork has been about.

I go to the basement, as per the snake's suggestion, gather up an armful of old dream journals and carry them upstairs. I see years' worth—pages and pages—of dream commentary on my spiritual life, psychological comings and goings, conversations, meetings, other wild adventures in many real and dream locations on this Earth. Dreams and more dreams, written and saved in a very large pile of color, image, story, drama, insight, and feeling. Sketches made frequently, capturing the color of it all.

I am amazed and humbled. What a collection and stupendous demonstration of the care and intelligence that flows from my own interior being out to my waking self. I have been fully supported and creatively led for years by this inner voice coming through the dreams. The state of my faith and trust in this inner guidance strengthens immediately.

The Soul of the Dawn Treader

Recently a dreamwork client described a little drawing she had made many times since she was a young girl. We decided to work it as a dream and to have her in good Gestalt fashion give a voice, thoughts, and feelings to the sketch as though it were a living entity. Amazing! She ended up in a powerful inner world that felt like her spiritual home, a castle in a kingdom of great beauty, safety, and creativity where she and her full powers reigned supreme as queen. She could return to this sanctuary in active imagination over and over again to experience her core strengths, values, and true nature.

As I thought of her work, I realized that I too had been regularly sketching a ship on the ocean since my earliest years. As a child growing up, I was in love with C.S. Lewis's *Chronicles of Narnia* and read the books over and over. Through my own active imagination, I met and loved the central Christ-like lion figure named Aslan. My spiritual outlook as a child was deeply impacted by this magnificent animal and his heroic adventures with the children in the books. Aslan himself tells the children that they have met and loved him so that in their world they would meet and know another like him, with a different name (meaning Christ). So at that time I began drawing the ship from his book, *The Voyage of the Dawn Treader,* and continued, without much thought, sketching it up into adulthood.

Husband Larry, an expert in facilitating active imagination, led me, as I had my client, in a process of stepping into the sketch and into the full, lively nature of this beautiful ship named the Dawn Treader.

I became her, spoke as her, and was simply dumbfounded at what came out.

I am made from fully alive, breathing wood, drenched by the depth and wisdom of the seas and her movements, and have an impeccable sense of direction through the seas and its interface with the continents. With great delight, I join in with people as they seek out their personal journeys. I offer my nautical wisdom to open and guide them into the adventures they need the most for their growth at that time.

As I spoke with the voice of this unusual and wise ship, I knew I was speaking my own heart's purpose as a dreamworker and visiting with others in their personal realms of dreams and imagination, helping them to see their own color, depth, and beauty; and to hear and know their own inner wisdom. And how I always delight in the many, many dream characters with whom I have had long conversations and the inner dreamscapes I have visited. That the strongest sense of my own nature and my life work came in the form of such an old, beloved, and delightful image felt like a gift from the Gods. Now I know, and as always, deeply appreciate the power and depth of active imagination, the creative communication of the soul as it does its visual storytelling.

I came to finally paint an image of the *Dawn Treader* several years ago. I did so with fondness, nostalgia even, but with no real awareness of what it meant to me, it ended up in storage. With a full heart, I recently carried the painting up from the dark basement and placed it near a sunny window in our living room where it could be seen and loved. This image ultimately found its way to the cover of this book.

A Pathway to Unity Vision

In my life, as you now know, there is an ongoing symposium filled with characters, entities, and creatures I have spoken with or become via dreamwork—my own and others. These are the most creative and surprising conversations ever. With rhinoceros, lions, skyscrapers, seashells, the sun, the city disaster, the baby, the monster living in the walls of a house, the car wreck, the elevator, the gypsy, the clock, and on and on the conversations go.

Do I not know all of them more deeply because I have walked in their shoes? Spoken their words? Would I not then move into, be open to seeing others in the waking world with voices and awareness just like my own? Magically emerging from this work is the grace-filled, golden, and powerfully loving perspective that everything and everyone has the same voice, is made of the same awareness. That there is only one beingness, awareness, consciousness, appearing in many different forms found inside our own bodies and outside in everything, from the sun to dandelions, to ants, birds, all people, to all the events in the waking world, and to all the dreams in the inner realms. Looking at the world through this pair of glasses expands our vision a thousand-fold and is a blessing and gift from Spirit.

Four-Leaf Clovers

As a small girl in elementary school, I recall having to stay home for the required six weeks with a spell of whooping cough. I shuffled around disconsolate and angry that one of my friends would get to take over my sidewalk patrol job helping kids cross the street, along with wearing *my* patrol badge. I went out to the backyard, where I found and picked a handful of four-leaf clovers. This, as I ate each and every one, would be how to change my luck and go back to school and my patrol route. Well, I got quite sick, and up they came, every last clover. In my thinking, I fully believed that I could seek, receive, and *take in* good fortune. Was this my first prayer to the higher power? I think so.

Church Camp

I went to church camp one summer when I was ten or eleven years old. One afternoon, the minister asked us to go out into a large grassy field, to pray and to experience God's presence. I obediently went out into the field, hopped up on a huge rock, and sat holding my head in my hands as I gazed out over the field. I waited and waited. Nothing happened. I was severely disappointed. Did I do this wrong? Was I given poor instructions? Was there anything there anyway? I was quite stirred up. I now believe that experience was the birth of strong questions and doubts about God's presence, and most especially, the beginnings of a longing for Spirit.

What was and is this search for the divine? Being broken-open, broken-hearted, or have one's heart filled with longing: a search that fully involves the heart. This journey of following longing where it leads could be my "further in and further up," my telling the tale of where I traveled next. Stay tuned.

Stop and Pause

We have completed a long, fascinating, expansive, challenging (maybe) journey through Dreamland, and have things to think about. Stop now and pause...... and breathe in and out, gently.... And imagine...

You are on the prow of the ship, wind in your face, facing outward over the wide sea, hand shading your eyes as you look ahead over the rolling waves.

Call forth and face into where the power of your own vision and inner explorations wish to take you. Invite those visions in, let them come up. Dream them up. Open up to your new direction and goals, and choose your means. What country will you stop in next? What journey will you make? What will you do, see, and learn? Write out and save all of the details, thoughts and images that arise from within.

Soon, make your plans.

ACKNOWLEDGEMENTS

To Larry: my beloved, deeply generous, and most witty companion in our shared life journey. My wish-fulfilling tree, inspiration, and shared heart, you have walked every step with me in this life, and conversed playfully with more of my dream entities than you ever wanted to! A newspaper man, researcher, and writer, you thoroughly represent the magic of the dictionary, as you edited this book from beginning to end and photographed all of my paintings.

To Bennie the Cat: Having a family member of another species is precious. Bennie, your curious mind and loving ways, padding around the bed in the middle of the night, or on your leash in the backyard sniffing and exploring. Your fascinating array of preferences (*only* clean towels for my bed, please) and ongoing communications nurtures my heart deeply.

To Rob Sanducci: A loving and wise healing presence for many years. You are a fellow dream traveler and loyal companion, generously sharing your profound wisdom and stunning personal adventures. Your clear vision always help me find my own unique way.

To Tammy, Haviva, Sara, Che, Rob, and Larry: Who, loving your dreams, wrote sparkling, touching, and evocative essays for *Sailing the Sea of Dreams*.

To Andrey Tamarchenko: Generously sharing your provocative life questions in our ongoing "gourmet" talks and a superb partner in our Dream Painting workshops. You are the art mentor who kindly and creatively supports my artist's heart. Your insights and collaboration helped create the book cover and other book paintings.

To Gerald May: You offered years of wise, funny, and loving spiritual guidance, always standing in a great, heartfelt love for God. Your words, teachings, and books are all washed through with discernment, delighted appreciation for the joy and conundrums of this life, and always is your tremendous good humor.

To Miss Chandler: My librarian as a child, you joyfully fed my youthful desire for adventure by stacking library books, including the *Chronicles of Narnia,* into my arms on a daily basis!

To Therese Bimka and Sally Schwager: Past directors of One Spirit, NYC Training Program for Spiritual Counseling and Ministry, for your inspired leadership, for the ongoing opportunity to work with and teach your students dreamwork, and for always including me in your warm-hearted ecumenical community.

To Tejasa: who has scrupulously prepared and creatively illustrated my dream material over the years. You have seen to my needs before I even know them and always found or created my favorite illustrations, including a child's head resting tenderly on the planet earth.

To Laura: a valued friend whose warm-hearted wisdom and refined skills managed the birth of this book's publication.

To: Carl Jung, Robert Johnson, Arnold Mindell, Jill Mellick, Strephon Kaplan Williams, authors, thinkers, healers, and teachers, whose teachings and books I have poured over and absorbed in my own work. Should any of your thinking be found accidentally unacknowledged in this book, you know why. Thank you for showing the way.

With profound ongoing gratitude: To Bhagavan Nityananda, Swami Muktananda, and Gurumayi Chidvilasananda for their radiant, transformative teachings guiding each and every day of my life.

Annotated Bibliography

Suggested Readings For Dreamwork Study

Castaneda, Carlos. *The Eagle's Gift*
> The continued tale of Castaneda's apprenticeship with teacher Don Juan.

Johnson, Robert. *Balancing Heaven and Earth*
> Autobiography by Jungian analyst and Episcopal priest, and author of many books about individuation. Exquisitely demonstrates a life lived in contemplation, with dreams/ inner work playing a foundational role.

Johnson, Robert. *Inner Work: Using Dreams and Active Imagination for Personal Growth*
> Direct, powerful ways of working with dreams and the unconscious by a master practitioner and Jungian analyst.

Johnson, Robert. *Owning Your Own Shadow: Understanding the Dark Side of the Psyche*
> Exploring, owning, and accepting the dark side of your personality.

Jung, C. G. *Memories, Dreams, Reflections*
> Autobiographical; conversations, writings, and lectures.

Ladinsky, Daniel. *I Heard God Laughing: Renderings of Hafiz*
> Heart-opening, heart-warming, and heart-breaking poetry by the Persian saint.

Lewis, C. S. *The Last Battle*

> The last book in the *Chronicles of Narnia,* following the adventures of the children from this world as they make their way in Narnia.

London, Peter. *Drawing Closer to Nature: Making Art in Dialogue with the Natural World*

> Full of useful and intriguing approaches for doing art in the natural world, along with wonderful advice for artists.

Luke, Helen. *Such Stuff as Dreams are Made On*

> Autobiography by Jungian analyst, a life devoted to community and the exploration of the Self, with dreams shared and woven into the commentary.

May, Gerald, MD. *Care of Mind, Care of Spirit*

> A classic in spiritual direction by psychiatrist and mentor to spiritual directors. Profound on issues of discernment between psychological and spiritual. Beautiful context for holding dreamwork.

Mellick, Jill. *The Natural Artistry of Dreams*

> Creative ways to bring the wisdom of dreams to waking life. A wonderful "How To" practical manual to explore your own dreams and to create dream processes for the people you work with.

Mindell, Arnold. *Working with the Dreaming Body*

> Revolutionary psychologist with his creative wife, Amy Mindell, propose the idea of the Dreambody, the inner voice trying to communicate with us through our dreams, body language, and relationships in order that we might live

fully whole and authentic. Fabulous. Also research online Arnold Mindell for further info on his work.

Mindell, Arnold. *Working on Yourself Alone*
Mindell gives strong exercises and processes for working personally on your own issues.

Ner-David, Haviva. *Dreaming Against the Current: A Rabbi's Soul Journey*
Author of an article in this book, Haviva tells stories of her spiritual and dream life.

O'Donohue, John. *The Four Elements*
A Celtic priest and poet, John writes of the profound nature of each of the four elements.

Sanford, John. *Dreams: God's Forgotten Language*
Jungian analyst and Episcopal priest, Sanford speaks eloquently of the healing nature of dreams, traces the treatment of dreams and visions in the Bible, and offers powerful perspectives for Christians in reconciling their dreamwork with their faith.

Swimme, Brian. *The Universe is a Green Dragon*
Written by a specialist in mathematical cosmology, his story of the beginnings of the universe and our Earth.

Tick, Edward, *The Practice of Dream Healing—Bringing Ancient Greek Mysteries into Modern Medicine*
The author uses case studies in actual trips to healing sites in the Greek islands, where people recreate the dream incubation ceremonies once held in ancient Greek temples.

Strephon Kaplan-Williams, *The Jungian-Senoi Dreamwork Manual: A step-by-step introduction to working with dreams.*

> The ultimate manual for over 30 dreamwork techniques, full explanations, a smorgasbord for the beginner or practiced dreamworker written by the former co-founder of the International Association for the Study of Dreams.

For further information about the role of dreams in other cultures, research: Native American Vision Quest; Dreams and Visions in the Christian Bible; Dream Temples and Dream Incubation in Ancient Greece; Aboriginal Dreamtime.

For further information about dreams, creativity, and understanding the dream, research the International Association for the Study of Dreams, with particular attention to Patricia Garfield and Jeremy Taylor.

ABOUT THE AUTHOR

Dr. Judith Schafman is a dream worker and spiritual director with a unique blend of spiritual and psychological perspectives based on Gestalt, Jungian, and Yoga principles. She has offered dream sessions, groups, trainings and workshops for many years.

Judith lives in the Catskill Mountains with her husband Larry and their marmalade cat, Bennie. She walks, paints, meditates and relishes her time in Nature. For more information about Judith's work, visit judithschafman.com

www.ingramcontent.com/pod-product-compliance
Lightning Source LLC
Chambersburg PA
CBHW051529120626
46551CB00012B/1141